IRISH HISTORY & MYTHOLOGY

Exploring the History, Celtic Myths, Folklore, Sagas, and Traditions of Ireland

HISTORY BROUGHT ALIVE

IRISH HISTORY AND MYTHOLOGY

© **Copyright 2023 - All rights reserved.**

Published 2023 by History Brought Alive

The content contained within this book may not be reproduced, duplicated, or transmitted without direct written permission from the author or the publisher.

Under no circumstances will any blame or legal responsibility be held against the publisher, or author, for any damages, reparation, or monetary loss due to the information contained within this book, either directly or indirectly.

LEGAL NOTICE:

This book is copyright protected. It is only for personal use. You cannot amend, distribute, sell, use, quote, or paraphrase any part, or the content within this book, without the consent of the author or publisher.

DISCLAIMER NOTICE:

Please note the information contained within this document is for educational and entertainment purposes only. All effort has been executed to present accurate, up-to-date, reliable, complete information. No warranties of any kind are declared or implied. Readers acknowledge that the author is not engaged in the rendering of legal, financial, medical, or professional advice. The content within this book has been derived from various sources. Please consult a licensed professional before attempting any techniques outlined in this book.

By reading this document, the reader agrees that under no circumstances is the author responsible for any losses, direct or indirect, that are incurred as a result of the use of the information contained within this document, including, but not limited to, errors, omissions, or inaccuracies.

FREE BONUS FROM HBA: EBOOK BUNDLE

Greetings!

First of all, thank you for reading our books. As fellow passionate readers of History and Mythology, we aim to create the very best books for our readers.

Now, we invite you to join our VIP list. As a welcome gift, we offer the History & Mythology Ebook Bundle below for free. Plus, you can be the first to receive new books and exclusives! Remember it's 100% free to join.

Simply scan the QR code to join.

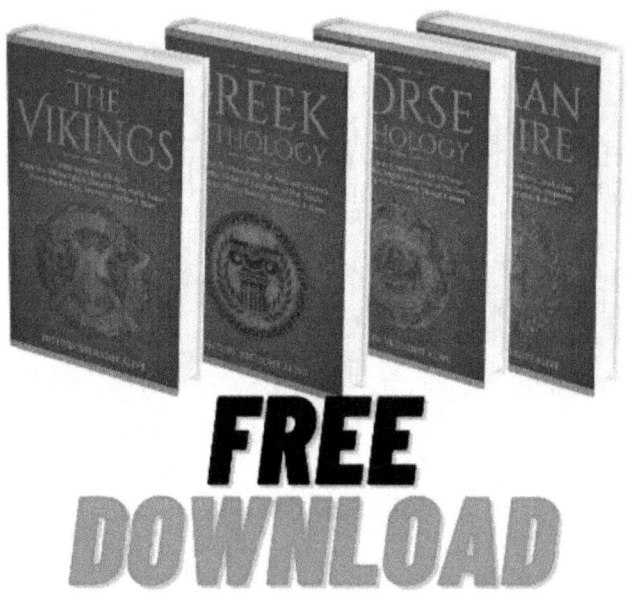

Keep up to date with us on:

YouTube: History Brought Alive

Facebook: History Brought Alive

www.historybroughtalive.com

CONTENTS

INTRODUCTION 1

CHAPTER 1: PREHISTORIC IRELAND 5

EARLIEST SETTLEMENT—THE MESOLITHIC AGE 5
Mount Sandel 8
NEOLITHIC ERA 9
Megaliths 13
THE CHALCOLITHIC AND BRONZE AGES 22
Legal System 24
THE IRON AGE 26

CHAPTER 2: GAELIC IRELAND 29

ARRIVAL IN IRELAND 32
THE LANGUAGE OF THE GAELS 33
POLITICAL DIVISION 34
LEGAL SYSTEM 35
RELIGION IN GAELIC IRELAND 39

CHAPTER 3: IRELAND DURING THE MIDDLE AGES 43

EARLY CHRISTIAN IRELAND 43
St. Patrick 44
Other Important Figures During This Era 45
VIKING AND NORMAN IRELAND 48
Early Vikings in Ireland 50
Norman Ireland 52

CHAPTER 4: IRELAND FROM THE RULE OF HENRY VIII 57

CHAPTER 5: IRISH PAGANISM 69

LEBOR GABÁLA 70
THE FOUR MYTHOLOGICAL CYCLES 74
THE OTHERWORLD 76
THE WHEEL OF THE YEAR 79

Imbolc.. *80*
Beltane..*82*
Lughnasa..*83*
Samhain *84*
Ostara..*86*
Litha *88*
Mabon *89*
Yule *90*

CHAPTER 6: MYTHOLOGICAL CREATURES .. 93

THE AOS SÍ...*94*
FAERIES *94*
   Leprechauns..*95*
   Pooka..*99*
   Banshee *101*
   Dullahan...*102*
   Leanan Sídhe..*103*
   Changelings..*103*
   Fachan *105*
   Cú Sidhe..*105*
   Cait Sí *106*
   Wyrm...*106*
   Demna Aeoir *108*
   Fear Gorta..*109*
   Alp Lauchra.. *110*
   Hags *111*
   Water Horse..*112*
   Man-Wolves of Ossory *113*
   Dwarves *114*
   Abhartach...*114*
   Dearg Due *115*
   The Questing Beast *116*
   Selkie...*117*
   Merrow..*117*
   Dobhar Chú *118*

Ellén Trechend *119*
Ghille Dhu..*119*
Féár Fortach *120*

CHAPTER 7: MYTHOLOGICAL FIGURES 123

THE TUATHA DÉ DANANN 123
   Danu *127*
   Dagda *127*
   Brigid... *129*
   Neit *130*
   Midir *130*
   Ainé..*130*
   Cermait..*131*
   Nechtan *131*
   Nuada *132*
   Boann *133*
   Aengus Óg *133*
   Morrigan *134*
   Manaanán mac Lir *136*
   Lugh... *137*
   Sovereignty *138*
   Étain *138*
   The (Potentially) Sacrificial Trio: Taranis,
   Teutates, and Esus *140*
   Dian Cécht *140*
   Bodach *141*
THE FIANNA 142
   Fionn mac Cumhail... *143*
GIANTS.. 143
   Amergin mac Eccit... *144*
   Iliach... *144*
   Dryantore... *144*
   Cú Chulainn... *145*
   Cú Roí mac Dáire.. *146*
FOMORIANS 147

Bres *147*
Domnu *148*
Balor *148*
Ethniu *148*

CONCLUSION **151**

REFERENCES **157**

INTRODUCTION

Ireland is a nation with a storied past. It's a nation that has roots going back 8,000 years—much of it unrecorded. The first written language in Ireland, Ogham, only started being used during the first millennium because the tribes of Ireland believed in the value of oral tradition. Even when the written word started being used, it wasn't an everyday affair as passing down knowledge in the form of stories was still the preferred way to educate. If you were driven to remember the things you were told, then it was believed that your mind would be strong and your capacity for retaining knowledge would be high.

This was effective, looking at the structures

that were built and other feats that were achieved based on orally transmitted knowledge. But it does make it difficult for people of the modern era to learn about life during prehistoric and ancient times. Luckily, a lot can be learned from the art, architecture, and other archeological remains that have been left by those that came before. Using this information, we've pieced together a comprehensive history of the island in this book.

A central point of Irish history is the mythology and beliefs that have been passed down from the Gaelic Pagan way of life. These myths have seeped into daily living and are a topic of conversation as common as talking about politics of the nation. Traditions and superstitions have been created around the creatures of myth, and these traditions are abided by without even thinking. In many cases, the myths and their creatures are just stories that we tell children before bed, but they have become integral to the identity of the nation.

This book examines the Pagan belief system, as it was then, and as it is now with Neopaganism. There is also an in-depth catalog of creatures of myth and characters of the supernatural. These sections both engage the mind and excite the imagination. The lives of the ancients were interwoven with the folklore imparted in this book, and it can be awe-inspiring to think that the creatures you read about have been part of the lives of people for hundreds, and sometimes thousands of years.

The last part of the book examines the impact of the history and mythology of Ireland on its two modern nations, The Republic of Ireland and Northern Ireland. The lives of those in modern rural areas and small towns place importance on what has been passed down by preceding generations. The lives of those in the largest urban areas, particularly Dublin, have often been influenced by international trends and lifted people away from their roots. One of the main purposes of this book is to allow you to reacquaint yourself with those roots and to allow you a glimpse into the identity of the Irish nation—a nation with a history stretching back thousands of years.

CHAPTER 1
Prehistoric Ireland

Preliterate Ireland didn't stretch as far back as some other prehistoric cultures. The earliest evidence of people in Ireland dates back to around 7 or 8,000 B.C.E. While there weren't written records of the time, and while written records that might have existed during the later prehistoric periods are lost or destroyed, a lot of information can be gleaned from archeological finds.

Earliest Settlement—The Mesolithic Age

The first settlers seem to have come to the island via the area of Coleraine in Northern Ireland. They seem to have crossed on a land bridge that had been extant at around that time and set up their first hunter-gatherer settlements. Another possibility is that they came to Ireland on wooden boats, landing in the region that now includes Antrim in the north of the island. There's an indication that the people who arrived in Ireland had come from Scotland because there were cultural similarities with the Scottish peoples of the time. It's possible that there was more than one crossing, on both land bridges and in boats. In addition to people crossing over, there's evidence that animals also crossed over on the land bridges of the time. There isn't much evidence of animals on the island before this time.

The era was called the Mesolithic Age. The Mesolithic Age refers to the earlier of the two stretches of the Stone Age; the other period being the Neolithic (or New Stone Age). In Ireland, the Mesolithic stretched from the arrival of the first people around 7 or 8,000 B.C.E., to around 4,000 B.C.E. (while it stretched back almost 200,000 years in some other places on the planet). This era was marked by a hunter-gatherer economy, the use of microliths (small flint pieces used in tools and weapons), and a meat-heavy diet. The population of Ireland mainly occupied coastal regions at first, particularly in the northern parts of the island.

As the period stretched on, they moved along the coast to the east and the south. There are indications that Mesolithic people went inland along some of the rivers, but not too far inland due to the heavily forested landscape of Ireland at the time. The hunter-gatherers moved from location to location, never permanently settling. They formed settlements where they went with wooden huts for each family that formed part of the tribe.

This continued until around 4,000 B.C.E. when the tribes started clearing away trees to make space for farming. Ireland was covered with thick forests at the time, which was ideal for hunting and gathering, but not for domesticated life. When trees were cleared off from an area, animal stock was reared and the ground was cultivated for raising cereal crops. These pastures and cultivated areas of land gradually grew in size, allowing for larger communities. One of the defining characteristics for the early agricultural and hunter-gatherer groups of Ireland were rituals where the body and objects were ceremonially painted. There were clear signs of an identifiable civilization emerging.

Mount Sandel

One settlement, Mount Sandel, is perhaps the earliest settlement of the era that's been uncovered and thoroughly examined by archeologists. The settlement seems to have been occupied for around half a millennium from approximately 7,000 B.C.E. The settlement consisted of round huts in which saplings had been bent and stuck into the ground to form a circle approximately 19 feet across. The saplings were covered with deer hides, thereby allowing protection from the elements.

There was a central hearth for the small community where the food that was caught would have been cooked and eaten communally. The settlement wasn't very large and could house 15 people at the most. The hearth would have been the central point for social interaction of the small community while they stayed warm next to the fire. In terms of food, those early settlers would have eaten multiple aquatic creatures, including shellfish, mackerel, eels, and the occasional seal. Land creatures would have included wild pig, deer, and game birds. A fish drying rack was found, which indicates that the Mesolithic inhabitants knew about food preservation by drying meat.

It is assumed that the main food eaten during the summer and other warm months was fish. Winter months likely had eel as the main dietary component, providing protein and omega-3 fatty acids. Plant components of the diet consisted of berries, fruit, and hazelnuts. Arrows, spears, and harpoons could be used to hunt fish and to kill other animals when meat was needed. The main land animal used for food would likely have been wild boars due to its prevalence at the time (being particularly useful as a food source in the cold winter months). The skins of animals that had been caught would have been used to clothe people in the village to keep them protected from the plants and creatures they walked past when entering the forest and providing warmth in the cooler parts of the year.

There are other archeological sites dated to the Mesolithic period in Ireland. The information gleaned from them is similar to those of the site at Mount Sandel—a lifestyle that largely consisted of roaming, a meaty diet, and use of small stone tools. The period that followed is the Neolithic Era.

Neolithic Era

This is the "New Stone Age" and stretches from approximately 4,000 to 2,000 B.C.E. in

Ireland. The period reached its height around 3,000 B.C.E., with large structures and lots of archaeological evidence left behind from this time.

The period started with waves of immigrants coming from the British Isles and beyond beginning in around 4,000 B.C.E. The native Mesolithic population was still present, but they were absorbed into the Neolithic population groups in some cases and displaced in other instances. The new population wasn't a hunter-gatherer society, but an agrarian one. They chopped and burned down the thinner forest layer close to the top of hills and created farmland on which to base their homesteads.

Along with farming came food security from the larger quantities of food available from farming, and because reserves could be stockpiled. To protect their homes and fields, the Neolithic farmers often built stone walls or other perimeter fencing around their homes and fields. With the introduction of cows, sheep, goats, and cereal grains from Britain, farmers could easily produce food each year within their protected fields. The homestead contained the houses for individual families and central buildings for communal affairs. With the protection in place and the farmland created, the dwellings were designed in a more permanent fashion for their residents. It was common for communities to consist of 20 to 30 people in multiple houses that each contained a family unit.

The houses were large and rectangular wood structures made from branches and trunks that were interwoven, with mud as a binding and insulating agent. Beams leaned against two sides of the structure's roof to provide additional support. The roof itself was made from thatch and reads to protect against the weather. There would often be a small opening in the roof that let out smoke because Neolithic people tended to cook inside their homes, rather than the exclusive use of a communal cooking point by Mesolithic communities. Cooking was done over a fire with meat put on a spit and smaller pieces put on a stone in the fire to fry on. Bread was likewise made on a stone placed in the fire using grain that had been ground from the harvest.

The difference between the stone tools of this era and the ones before were that the Neolithic tools were often larger, more detailed, and of a higher quality. Flint was still used, but porcellanite (found in Northern Ireland) was also introduced due to its added toughness.

Porcellanite was a useful material that was traded between Ireland and other lands, contributing to the trade and cultural interchange of the time. This included art, clothing styles, and more.

Coiled pottery was one of the forms of art commonly used in households at the time. When decorated, it could be a tool for imparting cultural elements from the tribe and incorporating elements from other tribes from whom ideas and goods had been accepted. This type of pottery was made by coiling clay around until it made the form of a pot, at which point it was smoothed out and decorations were added (using fingers, sticks, or stones as a decorative tool). The pot was then hardened in the fire, after which point it could be used for storage or to make lamps. When used as a lamp, it was filled with fat at the bottom, which was then lit when light was needed.

The security of life as the Neolithic period wore on resulted in a population increase. The population increase required more land for farming and living, thus driving people lower into the dense forests of the lowlands. To add to this, the change in climate and the use of the uplands for farming (with dead organic material forming peat) had resulted in some of the ground becoming bogs. As such, even established communities needed to move into the lower lying lands. They repeated the practice of deforestation in the regions where they needed to farm. As such, the island was now inhabited in the high and low areas, with the hills often becoming points of established, ceremonial importance.

Common cultural structures of Ireland and other European regions at this time were the large buildings that were created for social and burial purposes—also called megaliths—which were mainly found on the hills. Funerals and death were important to the culture of prehistoric Ireland, and these buildings were integral to many of those funerary practices. The next section will cover some of the main types found in Ireland.

Megaliths

Monuments are structures that tie together communities. They can be used to commemorate a part of the group's history or identity. Representing religious and spiritual beliefs is another purpose behind building monuments. The earliest known monuments in Ireland are more than 5,000 years old. This includes the Hill of Tara and passage of the tomb at Knowth. Both sites were used for burials and respecting the dead, among others.

There are many monuments in Ireland dating from the Stone Age (in excess of 1,500), particularly from the 4th millennium B.C.E. onwards. The cultural aspect that ties many of these monuments together can be seen in some of the art (such as swirling patterns) that occur at multiple locations. There are also similarities of design between some of the monument types. The types of monuments that can be found in Ireland include megaliths, dolmen, burial mounds, ringforts, and ceremonial grounds.

A megalith is a large stone that's placed upright, often with a ritualistic or culture-linked purpose. There are multiple formations that are used, including single standing stones (also called menhirs or gallauns), portal tombs, stone circles, court tombs, passage tombs, and wedge tombs. The purposes for the erection of megaliths are often as burial sites, to honor ancestors or important figures (such as deities, chiefs, or heroes), and to mark major achievements. The simplest of these, standing stones, aren't clear as to their purpose. They may have been used for any purpose ranging from rituals to cattle-rubbing posts to prevent damage to crops and fences. What can be said is that they are often humongous and taller than fully grown people.

Portal tombs, also called dolmen, are monuments that are made of two or more large stones holding up a capstone. The stones used are often extremely large, with the largest capstone in Ireland weighing over 150 tonnes. The dolmen often creates a passage or enclosure in the middle, which seems to have been used for ritualistic purposes in many cases. In some cases, they were used as burial locations, sometimes for many people over a period of hundreds of years. In other cases, it seems that they marked a ceremonial location for things such as feasts (likely feasts that honor ancestors or buried individuals). Then there are some dolmen where the purpose of the sight isn't clear at all. All that can be determined at those sights are that many people expended large amounts of effort to create a monument that's still standing thousands of years later.

Stone circles can be found all over Ireland, particularly near the coast. They are a common feature in many western European ancient societies but are particularly common on the Emerald Isle and in the UK. There is much debate as to their actual purpose because there isn't any written record from the preliterate societies that constructed them. That said, there are a few common assumptions that archeologists use. The first is that they were constructed as time markers or calendars of some sort. This holds credence in that there are many stone circles that mark the passage of the sun and show when it's the summer solstice, one of the two equinoxes, among other dates.

Then there's the hypothesis that they were used for religious and cultural ceremonies. One particular type of indication as to the veracity of this theory is that multiple stone circles have a dolmen in the center that was used as a burial site. It's not too much of a stretch to say that the sites were thus used for worshiping and healing. But the popular idea that stone circles were constructed for the use of druids and their worshiping or healing practices is likely not true, considering that the preponderance of the stone circles were constructed thousands of years before the arrival of the Gaels in Ireland. The earliest ones that we know of were constructed in the 4th millennium B.C.E.—perhaps even earlier.

A final possibility that's commonly advanced is that stone circles were gathering places for their communities. This would have made them centers of trade, as well as sites of social gatherings. The link between the marking of important agricultural events (due to the motion of the moon and sun) would have made the stone circles a useful device for farmers in those communities. Whatever they were actually used for, there's no denying that stone circles still capture the imagination of many thousands of years after they were made.

A court tomb, also known as a court cairn (due to the piles of rocks within the perimeter stones), is a collection of megaliths or stones that forms a court. The structure has four sides (usually with two long sides that are somewhat equivalent in length and two shorter sides that aren't equal in length) and often has more than one chamber inside. There's a semicircular entrance hall or forecourt on the one side of the court (usually at the larger of the two short sides of the structure). To keep the structure in place, there is orthostat (large stone slabs placed on their sides) or dry stone (walls made by stacking stones without adhesive materials) that forms a perimeter around smaller rocks on both the outside of the court and the chambers on the inside of the court. There were roofs on top of the court cairns that were held up by overlapping stones or by forming corbels (stone structures that jut out of a wall to support a roof) to hold up the roof.

Court tomb might have been a misnomer for these buildings because there are few with evidence of burials or human remains. Those that have evidence mainly contain remnants of cremations that were carried out in the court. The preponderance of evidence from the size and formation of these constructions show that they would have made effective locations for gathering people, whether it was to hold weddings, initiations, religious gatherings, or for civic purposes. There are still remains of many court cairns (more than 400) in Ireland—mainly in the northern half of the island.

Passage tombs, also called burial mounds, are made up by a collection of structural elements. There are chambers in the center wherein rites could take place. The chamber is connected to the outside world by a passage. The entrance to the passage is of a sturdy design, sometimes with large stones holding it up. There's a large mound of earth placed over it all. In the central chamber you might find things such as basins and motifs or other designs.

In the Newgrange, there is a high ceiling in the chamber that goes about 13 feet high. It also allows sunlight to pass through the passage on winter solstice for a few minutes, thus illuminating the inner chamber and indicating the approaching new year. These sites are sometimes surrounded by kerb stones (large stones with special designs and patterns etched onto their surface that were used to prop up the earth and grass of the mound) and cairns (man-made piles of stones). The kerb stones are still of keen interest to archeologists who are trying to understand their meaning. In some instances, the designs on the kerb stones seem to change their shape and significance based on variations of light and shadow.

A structure that's more common in the west of Ireland than the other parts of the island is the wedge tomb. This is a type of stone structure where multiple stones are used as walls that hold up a roof of stone slabs—the roof slabs, in turn, being covered with cairns (stacks of smaller stones). The walls and roof taper to form a wedge-like shape (hence the name). The opening, which is at the larger side of the tapering rock structure, faces the direction of the setting sun—west or south-west. Further, they are mainly found on the sides of hills, normally about two-thirds of the way up their respective hill. They are often used to house remains (sometimes for more than one person), whether cremated or buried, along with tools and pottery. These tombs started being constructed around 2,500 B.C.E., thus they are the newest category of Stone Age monument to be constructed in Ireland, yet this didn't make them any less popular than other Stone Age monuments with around 400–500 of them extant.

Ring forts have been made at different times throughout Irish history and are one of the most common historical structures on the island, with more than 40,000 that are known about. There were ones made during the Stone and Bronze Ages—called fairy forts. Then there are ones that were made during the Middle Ages. Those made during the Middle Ages were mainly the round foundational remnants of wood or stone homes that housed farming families. These homes are called ring forts because they were commonly surrounded by a bank, either of stone or earth, with a ditch directly outside of it. There was an entrance with a gate where inhabitants could enter and exit the home's property.

The older version, fairy forts, served essentially the same purpose. They were the location of prehistoric homes and forts that housed farming families and could be used to protect those families and their stock. There were ridges and ditches, sometimes multiple concentric rings of them, that surrounded the family building or compound. Many of these had an underground storage location, which came to signal entrances to the Otherworld in Irish mythology. The flee of the godlike race, the Tuatha Dé Danann, to the Otherworld in folktales was linked to the ditches that were found in the ground of these fairy forts. A holy significance was thus attached to these sights, resulting in great reverence being directed to them.

The actuality of their original construction was far less glamorous. The fairy forts—also called lios, rath, and cashels—were homes and fortifications of wood, stone, or mud that were surrounded by wooden fences and earthworks. Their purpose was to keep livestock in and to keep out danger in the form of predators and raiders.

A similar structure used for an entirely different purpose was a ring-barrow. These were locations where bodies or cremated remains were buried. They were sites that started to be raised during the Stone Age, but continued to be used until the Iron Age, i.e., were used until around 600 B.C.E. They were made by placing a ditch and raised band of earth around a grave—usually a single grave rather than a grave for multiple people. These vary from barrows (also called tumuli) in that barrows consisted of a pile of earth (or rocks) placed over a body to form a small hill-like structure.

The purpose of a barrow could also be broader than a ring-barrow since a barrow could house multiple bodies or could be a marker for a cemetery. Some barrows had an entrance and most of them had a ditch that formed a ring around the tumulus's mound. There's been some debate, but it is thought that a barrow was an indication of the buried person's social status. This is partly because there are sites with multiple barrows, some being larger than others, as well as other moundless graves (either in the form of cists, stone boxes, or earth-cut graves). As a note, a cist is a hole built in the ground (often lined with wood or stone) in which remains are kept.

The next period, the Copper Age, was a period when there was less construction of large stone tombs and buildings. The focus had shifted to smaller structures and underground places of burial. The same can be said for the Bronze Age, which followed directly after. The next section will give you an overview of life in Ireland during these periods.

The Chalcolithic and Bronze Ages

The Chalcolithic Age, also called the Copper

Age, was the transition point between the Stone and Bronze Ages. There were many copper and gold deposits in Ireland during prehistoric times. It was one of the higher yielding copper producers in ancient Europe. The copper was mined, then the ore was transported to be smelted and molded. In earlier times, the techniques to smelt and mold weren't highly developed, which meant that much of the earlier copper tools were made by shaping cooler copper with hammering tools. The Copper Age of Ireland started at around 2,500 B.C.E. and reached its height at around 2,000 B.C.E., relatively on par with the time of the Bronze Age.

The Bronze Age was a further advancement of the developments of implements in the Copper Age. Smiths realized that by making an alloy with tin, they could produce stronger implements—seeing that copper was quite soft. Due to the lack of tin in Ireland, Cornwall became a strong trading partner because of its large tin mining operations—with Ireland trading gold and copper for the tin. The importing made it expensive at first, which is why some parts of Ireland didn't have much of a Bronze Age before the introduction of the Iron Age. The Bronze Age officially lasted from around 2,600 B.C.E. to 2,100 B.C.E., making it a relatively short archaeological period. That said, there were many developments that took place in this time.

Stone tools were still used in some circumstances (e.g., hammers) since it was cheaper to access than metals. That said, the stone tools that were produced were of a higher quality, and in some cases more decorative elements were added. The techniques that had been developed from the start of the Stone Age made it easy to produce high quality stone tools at a low cost. There were, however, a few things that made metal tools more desirable because stone shattered when hit against something too hard while metal didn't. And even if it did get damaged, it could be altered back into shape or re-cast into another usable form. Additionally, copper and bronze tools could be made a lot sharper than stone ones.

Legal System

The legal system of prehistoric Ireland passed along orally due to the lack of a writing system. The legal system was largely carried over into written form when Christianity arrived in Ireland in the 5th century A.C.E. The thousands of years prior to that may have had many alterations to the law, but it can be assumed that much of the legal structure of the communities was the same.

The society of prehistoric Ireland was largely tribalistic, meaning that there were many tribes that owed allegiance to each other and were self-governed. Those tribes had a few officials, such as a king and a judge, that upheld the laws of their people. The tribes around them would have had their own judges and kings and officials. Remedies for legal problems were mainly imposing fines or compensating the victim or their families, whatever the cause of the legal situation. There wasn't a distinction between civil and criminal law, so whatever the type of situation where the wrongdoing occurred, the victim or their family would approach the relevant official to have the dispute adjudicated. An appropriate fine or other form of compensation would then be levied against the wrongdoer.

The person who heard the case would make an independent decision as to the relevant compensation. The judge, or king or other official holding court, would hear out the case presented to them and make a decision they deemed fair based on the laws they were taught orally. There wasn't interference from other individuals and there wasn't a jury. The king or judge was seen as holding the authority of the law. They were the embodiment of the law, which meant they were neither above it nor subject to it. In addition to the protection that law offered, religion was also important as a guidance in matters of survival and morals.

The Iron Age

The Iron Age was the period when iron started being used in larger quantities. It had been used in multiple locations around the world during the Bronze Age, but it wasn't particularly harder than bronze, so there wasn't any reason to incorporate it into society on a large scale yet. The innovation of adding carbon and other ingredients to make steel is when it started becoming more popular because steel was harder than bronze. When you put it through the process of quenching (rapidly cooling it from a heated state by dunking it in things such as water or oil), the steel becomes even harder. Add to this the fact that you can cast iron (and steel) and that iron is the fourth most abundant element in the Earth's crust, then you have a winning combination that made this the material for tools of the day. It's still one of the most popular materials for tools to this day.

The Iron Age in Ireland was dominated by the Celts, to whom the next chapter will be dedicated.

CHAPTER 2
Gaelic Ireland

The Celts were an ethnic, linguistic, and socio-economic group that stretched across much of northern Europe and Asia Minor during the last parts of the Bronze Age and through the Iron Age. The Celts had a rapid period of expansion during their height in the 5th to 1st centuries B.C.E. Before we look at how they relate to the Gaels of Ireland and how they were involved with Irish development, first we're going to look at a few key characteristics of Celtic culture and lifestyle.

The Celts wore clothes made of natural fibers (usually linen and wool, but sometimes silk or hemp). They also used leather and fur for the durability and protection against the elements offered by both. The clothing worn by people of Celtic communities were matters of great pride, sometimes taking more than a month to make a single article of clothing. The clothes were usually in the forms of robes, dresses, tunics, and skirts for both men and women. These items were often brightly colored with the natural colorants available at the time (even stale urine in some cases for its yellow color). Adorning yourself with jewelry, headbands, and feathers was also popular as it showed wealth and status in addition to acknowledging religious beliefs in some cases.

The society of the Celts was male dominated, yet women could hold positions of importance in both official and social capacities. These positions included things like ambassadorship, warriors, and kings. Social standing often had to do with the wealth of the individual woman concerned, which she could get from inheriting, work, or as gifts from her husband. Jewelry such as necklaces, rings, and bracelets were the prime way to show your wealth and cement your social standing, along with embroidery.

The religion of the time varied from Celtic tribe to Celtic tribe. While there was much similarity in the religious beliefs of the tribes (such as pantheistic worship and acknowledgement of the importance of nature or natural features), each tribe had its own gods and variations for popular rites. The religious beliefs of the tribes influenced how they created art, with much of the art being in the form of patterns and shapes, but some of it showing humanoid figures (often with animal parts). These figures were normally deities that were honored as both a sign of respect and as a way to show wealth. Art came in the form of jewelry, stonework, embroidery, goldsmithing, and designs on household objects (such as clay lamps).

The government of the Celts was fractured in much the same way as their religion. While there were kings that held authority over large numbers of people, a better description would be to say that the Celts were a mixture of tribes that had authority over themselves. Each tribe had its own ruler and structure to protect the population and levy tax. Things that brought multiple tribes together included hunting, defense against opposing ethnic groups, trading, and religious worship or major festivals. Thus, despite each tribe being self-governing to some extent (even if there was an external king that had higher authority than their local chief), they were still incorporated with other Celtic tribes that might have been very distant from their own location.

The Celtic population groups that are found in the British Isles include the Gaels and the Brythonic. The Gaels were the Celts that had originally landed in Ireland and occupied it during the Iron Age, while the Brythonic were the Celts who had originally settled Britain during the same era. There was warfare between these two subsections of the Celts since that era, resulting in migration of both population groups. The Celtic populations of Ireland, Scotland, and the Isle of Man are the descendants of the original Gaels; and the Celtic populations of Wales, Cornwall, and Brittany are the descendants of the Brythonic. The rest of the Celtic tribes and population groups have majorly been absorbed into other cultures and population groups since the invasions of the Ancient Romans into the rest of Europe.

Arrival in Ireland

The Celts arrived in Ireland around 500 B.C.E. It's assumed that they arrived over a period of hundreds of years, gradually spreading throughout the island and mixing in with the native population of the Bronze, Copper, and Stone Ages. Celtic language and culture spread with them, as it had done throughout northern Europe, Britain, and beyond. The language was used in oral form and written records weren't really made use of until the 4th century A.C.E., although some examples have been found originating in the first century A.C.E.

The Language of the Gaels

Oral tradition was used to pass down cultural knowledge and history, medicinal and craft knowledge, and anything else of significance to the Gaels at the time. It was said that some druids were able to keep entire catalogs of medicinal plants in their mind, thereby providing professional care to the ill that came to them for aid.

When the written language came into use, it wasn't used for long texts, but rather for short inscriptions on a number of signs and monuments (such as tombs). The written language of the Gaels was called Ogham, and it consisted of lines and nicks cut into a surface, with 1 to 5 lines for each letter. Ogham was used in Ireland until around the 8th century A.C.E., when the Roman language, as used in the Christian faith and influences of other languages from trade partners, altered the written language practices.

Political Division

The society was divided into finte, which were communities with a king at their top. Patrilineal descent was the order of the day, so male descendants would inherit land and responsibilities from the deceased king or relatives. The descent could also include fostered children in some cases, meaning you could inherit certain things even if you weren't related by blood, but rather by adoption. The society was further divided beyond the family you came from. It was a hierarchical society with its own caste system. There were the unfree, the free, the doernemed, and the soernemed.

The unfree were slaves. They had to provide work at no cost. They could not own possessions nor land, and they passed on their unfree status to their children.

Freemen was a dual category. There were the free who were poor and owned little to nothing, yet they were treated better than the unfree. There were also the freemen who held possessions and land, thus gaining social and political status in their communities. This higher tier of freemen could qualify as a briugu if they elected to open their homes to others. If they held this role, they would have to provide food and shelter to anyone who came, up to the capacity of their home. This came with benefits on both a social level and in relation to the freeman's political and legal rights.

The doernemed were the professionals of Gaelic society. They were physicians, legal representatives, poets, historians, and craftspeople. These positions required study and practice, and they could be passed on to your descendants. Particularly skilled doernemed were classified as ollam. They were sponsored by wealthy individuals and families, gaining much more financial freedom and personal status than others lower than them on the hierarchy.

Soernemed were the top caste and consisted of chiefs, kings, highly skilled poets, druids, and their families. These individuals had powers to rule and had large collections of resources. Each position had a different role that was essential to the identity and sovereignty of its tribe.

Legal System

The legal system of the Gaels was called Brehon Law, and it remained in influence until more than a thousand years after Ireland had converted to Christianity. In fact, some parts of Brehon Law are still in force to this day, even if in altered form. The main causes of alteration were the introduction of Christianity, Norman rulership, English rule, and modern changes for the law to suit society's needs. Original Brehon Law applied to all parts of life and was uniformly applicable, even to the kings.

One of the main characteristics of the original legal system was that criminal and civil matters were treated and remedied as one—there was no distinction. When a transgression was committed against someone, the main remedy was to provide them (or their dependents) with compensation to take care of any financial needs of the injured party. The focus wasn't on punishing the perpetrator, but on providing for the victim. If the victim had been murdered, for instance, their family would be provided with funds from a fine that was levied against the murder. If the fine couldn't be paid, then the murderer would either be enslaved, waiting until the killer could pay the fine, or killing the murderer.

The situation was similar if you harmed someone physically. In this case, you would consult your victim's attorney or the victim directly and determine how much would be an appropriate payment to compensate for the wound. This needed to include the price of accommodation, food, and care. The fee would vary depending on the part of the body that was wounded (with the highest fines being for body parts that could lead to death), how intensely it was damaged, which would be determined by a doctor upon inspecting the patient. Further, the wrongdoer would need to take care of their victim while they were recovering. The matter of intention when causing the wound held a lot of importance, as well as actions done by the victim that contributed to their injury.

Inheritance was another matter of importance in Brehon Law. It dictated that the property you inherited also came with added responsibilities and expectations, depending on the social standing that it gave you. For instance, if you inherited the family lands, you would also inherit the responsibility that came with maintaining those lands for the benefit of the rest of the family. If a person inherited the status of the head of the family, he would also have to care for the widows of the family and pay the debts of those he was responsible for if they couldn't pay it themselves. If the person refused to take on the responsibilities due with the inheritance, then they would forfeit the property and position (and would possibly be kicked out of the family altogether). Men could inherit any type of property, depending on their closeness to the deceased (in terms of biological relationship), and the order of their birth.

Women, on the other hand, were only able to inherit money.

The law was also concerned with the treatment of women. While men generally held senior positions and could hold more types of property than women, women could still hold high positions (such as queen) and seek justice for wrongs that were committed against them. An example of this was divorce or financial compensation if a woman's husband beat her up too heavily while disciplining her or if he heavily abused her. That said, a husband could beat up his wife to "correct" her behavior. In terms of property, the marriage joined both the husband and wife's possessions, but they could be separated back in some cases.

Finally, Brehon Law regulated the ranks and functions of kings. There were three levels of kings. The bottom level was in charge of a single tuath (or kingdom). The next highest level would hold power over multiple tuaths or tribes. While the final rank was known as the king kings or the high king and had authority over all people in the region. This meant that they would provide governance for all those people, embody the laws of the region, provide judgements, lead ceremonies, and perform other official roles. If they didn't perform their functions properly or were injured (i.e. if they didn't possess the quality of kingliness), then they would be replaced with an alternative king. As such, the king did hold the highest political power in their land, but they were on par with the law, not above it.

Religion in Gaelic Ireland

The Celts in general had different religions from tribe to tribe. This was the same with the Gaels. Each group had their own deities, heroes, and beliefs. That said, there were common denominators among the Gaelic religions, the chief of which was that there were gods in each to embody the most important parts of nature and the most important characteristics of human life, such as love. As such, there were hundreds of gods, but they weren't all uniformly worshiped in Ireland—save a few of the most important and established ones.

Another common denominator of Gaelic religions was the belief in the animation of inanimate objects. Rocks, trees, mountains, and a number of other natural features were all believed to have a soul, and thus to be worthy of respect. Even though things such as rocks were lifeless, their similarities with humans and animals (such as endurance in dealing with environmental stresses) were noted and admired. The nature of those objects (such as rivers) and of animals were carried into the descriptions and identity of the gods in any given religion of the Gaels. This was occasionally carried to the extent where ownership was disallowed of certain natural features due to the divine nature associated with it.

Another aspect of Gaelic religion was that religious tolerance was not only allowed but was encouraged. In other words, the trade partners and the foreigners living in lands owned by the Gaels were allowed to practice their own religions. This didn't only relate to beliefs, but also related to ceremonies and rituals. When Christianity became popular in Ireland, it was easily assimilated into the Gaelic population due to their comfortable acceptance of people of all beliefs. Soon Christianity became the majority religion, once it was figured out how to incorporate some of the core pagan beliefs and practices into the traditional Christian ones. While this was a challenge due to Christianity being monotheistic, it was managed through such practices as making some of the Gaelic gods into saints who had performed miracles and incorporating Gaelic festivals into the Christian calendar, albeit with alterations).

In the next chapter we will explore Ireland

during the Early Christian Period in which St. Patrick lived, and the Viking period that followed.

CHAPTER 3
Ireland During the Middle Ages

The Middle Ages in Ireland was a period full of changes and invasions. This chapter looks at the most important historical changes of this period, right up to the reign of King Henry VIII.

Early Christian Ireland

Christianity came to the British Isles with the Roman Empire, which had itself converted to Christianity as the chief religion in the early 300's A.C.E. First it had been accepted with the Edict of Milan, after which it openly became the most important religion of the empire. This spread to the British Isles, where it had become a popular religion with the locals of England. The English locals were often captured by the Irish as slaves, and those slaves are believed to be the first individuals to bring Christianity to Ireland. Those slaves would share the faith with the people they came into contact with, resulting in a basic understanding and burgeoning acceptance of the religion. The first major conversion, however, is said to have been brought about by the patron saint of Ireland, St. Patrick.

St. Patrick

Saint Patrick was born to a family in England that was under the rule of the Roman Empire during the fifth century A.C.E. He lived comfortably until his capture by Irish bandits when he was 16, at which point he was taken to Ireland. While there, he was taken into slavery and held the position of managing flocks and herds of animals. This went on for several years until he secured an escape back to England on a ship. Once he reached England, he had trouble getting to his family due to hunger and incarceration along the way. Eventually he reached them, at which point they sent him to Europe for training as a religious leader.

He completed his training and was ordained. While there, he received letters from the

Christians in Ireland requesting that he go to them and help with efforts to convert the land. He later accepted this offer and sailed to the land to start with ministering and converting en masse. He baptized people and carried out confirmations. Interactions with political and royal powers were also important to create goodwill, so he provided gifts to officials and required no gifts in return.

People knew him as a miracle worker, allegedly raising people from the dead, providing provisions using the power of prayer alone, making snakes leave Ireland, and causing a herd of pigs to appear, among other feats. There are also stories in which he battled mythical beasts to protect those of the local population. With the work he did and the miracles he performed, he was one of the most influential early Christians and he is lauded as the individual that converted Ireland to make it a Christian land.

Other Important Figures During This Era

The early Christian era of Ireland lasted from around 400 to 800 A.C.E. (with St. Patrick believed to have lived and worked in Ireland during the 400s).

Saint Brigid of Kildare was one of the other

two patron saints of Ireland, along with Saint Columba. She was born to a slave and a noble (in the fifth century A.C.E.), with her dad selling both her and her mom to a druid early on in life. While under the ownership of the druid, she remained devout to her Christian faith, even managing to convert him. He gave her back to her father due to his respect for her, at which point her father tried to sell her to a king in Ulster. She once again showed her devoutness, and the king granted her freedom from parental care and slavery as a sign of respect.

She performed works of devotion and got the attention of a king in Leinster, who provided her with a plain in Kildare to build the first nunnery in Ireland. The nunnery was successful, leading to her establishing more over the succeeding years. All the while she continued with her work of conversion and performing miracles, such as providing enough beer for a colony of lepers from to barrels that had originally been filled with water. Some say she is merely the Christianization of a figure that had originally existed as a deity in the Pagan faith, while others say she was a born and real woman who became a saint. Whichever the case may be, her legacy has resulted in a permanent mark on Ireland.

Saint Columba, also known as Columcille,

was born in 521 A.C.E. and came from an ancestry of royals. He was devout from an early age, studying and becoming an ordained priest. He was an influential figure, founding the towns of Durrow and Derry, and founding Christian communities across Ireland, Scotland, northern England, the Inner and Outer Hebrides, and the Orkney Islands. He had a storied life that provided guidelines to many. The story started with a squabble over a valuable book of Psalms, a book which he had secretly copied without the approval of its owner.

When the owner found out about it, he brought the matter before their king to adjudicate the dispute. The king declared that both the original book and the copy that had been made (the copy still existing today in the ownership of the O'Donnell clan) would go to the owner, and that St. Columba would be imprisoned. The saint broke out of the prison and caused warfare to break out when he incited his kinsmen and followers with the story of his mistreatment by the king. The warfare was violent and resulted in the death and injury of many people. The saint felt horrible for the destruction that had been created in connection with him, so he voluntarily exiled himself and a group of his followers to the island of Iona as penance.

Not being satisfied with sitting and feeling sorry for himself, the saint was a man of action. He built a church on Iona, and it would become the mother church of all the others he would go on to found in the British Isles. His churches and monasteries were places of learning and of faith. The sheer amount of change he brought about by founding these churches and training others to spread the faith is why he is known as one of the three patron saints of Ireland.

The Early Christian period lasted for a few hundred years. It was a period when many conversions took place, making Christianity the main faith of the island. Religious buildings became centers of religious, social, and commercial life, with some of the monasteries becoming the leaders of scholastic education for the whole European continent. The High Kings converted to Christianity and Paganism was absorbed into the Christian faith.

The era came to an end when the Vikings started invading and establishing themselves as a force to be reckoned with.

Viking and Norman Ireland

The Vikings were seafaring warriors who exerted their influence on much of Europe due to their military prowess. They originated in Scandinavia and were originally thought to be an agricultural people. The combination of their large population (possibly overpopulation in relation to their resources), their superior strength, and their above-average fighting ability led them becoming raiders of the lands surrounding them.

The societal classification system of the Vikings had landowners (the chiefs) at the top, who would provide land to clan heads, freemen, and retainers (the servants or laborers of the other classes). In other words, land ownership was a prime determinant of social standing. But, with the rise of the Viking population, there was demand placed on further expansion and conquering of surrounding regions. The populations of the Viking lands (mainly present-day Scandinavia) had become too large and powerful to remain complacent with the land they already had. Raiding was the solution to this situation.

Raids would normally entail traveling in a longship to a region with reasonable resources. This would be followed by striking the region, fighting and killing where necessary to subdue the population of the village or town. Once subdued, resources would be plundered, then buildings, trees, lands, or infrastructure would be burned. This whole process would be quite fast due to the strategy being to strike, take, and leave. This earned the Vikings a reputation of piracy, hence them being given the name víkingr, which meant "pirate" in a few historical Scandinavian languages.

Early Vikings in Ireland

During the 700's A.D., the Vikings started successfully raiding the Irish coast and up its rivers. Their main targets were monasteries and religious buildings where high value goods were held with minimum protection. They established strongholds on the Irish coast from where they could maintain their fleets and establish trade routes within and outside of Ireland. The strongholds were the towns of Cork, Dublin, Limerick, Waterford, and Wexford—all of which were fortified by the Vikings for their protection against the locals. In addition to the valuables, materials, and food they obtained on their raids, the Vikings established a slave trade where they would capture native Irish and sell them for financial gain.

Despite the power of the Vikings and their influence on the trade routes of Ireland, they weren't able to capture kingdoms, despite the political landscape of the island being highly fragmented. This was mainly because there was a large ruling class due to the decentralized nature of the kingdoms, and because there could be multiple successors for each king. In other words, when a king was killed (or even their entire family), they could just be replaced by the next most eligible native successor, thereby leaving no power vacuums and preventing anarchy. As such, the Irish were able to maintain their independence everywhere except for the Viking coastal strongholds, and even these would come to fall under Irish control once again.

In the late 900's, the high king Brian Boru led forces against the strongholds of the Vikings. Unlike previous attempts to take control of the Viking-controlled parts of Ireland, Brian Boru's attempts were successful. First his forces captured Limerick, followed by the capture of Cork, Wexford, and Waterford. The most powerful stronghold, Dublin, would come under his control, which briefly caused the Viking population of the town to retreat. The high king was killed shortly after the retreat took place, but the effects of the warfare were permanent. The Vikings who had been incorporated into the Irish landscape could no longer take what they wanted without backlash. Rather, they were allowed to continue trade and to participate in the civil affairs of the Irish (even intermarrying and having children), but in a capacity similar to fellow countrymen.

Norman Ireland

The Normans were the Vikings who had raided and taken over the land that resides around northwestern France at present. The area had been raided by Vikings, who subjugated much of the local Frankish-Celtic people. The king of West Francia (a kingdom that occupied much of what is today the western third of France) formed a treaty with the leader of the Viking invaders, Rolo, in which they would take control of part of West Francia (in the region that is today known as Normandy), in exchange for protecting the local population and converting to Christianity. Rolo and his Viking subjects kept their promise, mixing with the Frankish-Celtic population of the region during the 10th and 11th centuries C.E. and becoming known as the Normans.

During the 11th century C.E., William the Conqueror (a Norman leader) expanded the power of his nation by taking the English throne. This made the Normans the most powerful political force in the British Isles, leading to incursions on Ireland soon after. The final blow was in 1169 when the Norman crown in England took control over large parts of

Ireland under the approval of the Pope of Rome. The Pope disagreed with the way Christianity was practiced in Ireland, thus consenting to the island's subjugation by the Normans in return for stricter compliance with Roman Catholic practices among the island's population.

The result was the Angevin Empire, which consisted of half of France, all of England, and parts of both Wales and Ireland. Irish politics were brought under the control of the Lordship of Ireland. The Lordship continued even when the French took control of the regions falling under the Angevin Empire from the Normans over the 13th and 14th centuries. Ireland thus remained officially under English control for centuries, despite political changes that happened in the larger nation during that time.

At the start of this period, there was a big focus on expanding the agricultural and commercial sectors of Ireland. This was sped along by the establishment of many towns, hundreds of churches, and plenty of castles around the island.

While the Normans held strict control in parts of Ireland, they couldn't maintain their command. This was partly due to a lack of direct involvement from the kings in England, but perhaps more because the governing system incorporated in Ireland was disorganized. The local Irish didn't need the organized structures of the Normans to be successful, thus they held their own without the need for assistance from a strict governing structure. The Normans were absorbed into the Irish population by intermarriage as a result, at least in the areas beyond the Pale.

The 13th century marked the real turning point of real power of the island. During the 13th century, many of the local Irish lords started conflicts with pure Norman-backed lords. A strategy that was particularly effective was surprise attacks to take resources and cause havoc. Further, some of the Norman lords started getting greedy or strapped for resources, resulting in infighting, which made it easier for the Irish to overpower them. The Irish and Irish-Normans were thus able to take control back from many of the less significant English nobles.

The 14th century had even more of a power shift with the occurrence of the Black Death and the distraction of English monarchs by the War of the Roses. The Irish populations of the island were able to withstand the dire effects of the Black Death better due to a more spread-out rural population than the loyal English living on the island. The close-living of the English in towns such as Dublin resulted in the plague both spreading faster in those areas and taking longer to stop affecting those areas. As such, the population of towns was more heavily reduced than that of rural areas.

As for the lack of financial and military support from the English crown due to their concern with the War of the Roses, the result was that Irish lords and those loyal to their cause were more capable of attacking and taking control of areas that they previously weren't able to—particularly since the lordship of Ireland had been delegated to a powerful family that had resided in England for more than a century (the Fitzgeralds of Kildare). In the end, there were very few areas outside of Dublin where real control was in the hands of the English. This all changed after the rule of Henry VIII.

CHAPTER 4
Ireland From the Rule of Henry VIII

The control of the English monarchs had waned until the 16th century, with the little control that remained being centered around Dublin and surrounding areas in the Pale. When Henry VIII was crowned and made general and king, he gradually took more steps to take control of the island nation. The first was to appoint Gerald Fitzgerald (the Earl of Kildare at the time) as his deputy to hold the lordship of Ireland. Gerald had shown that he was a powerful man and he had great ambition.

The appointment proved to be problematic in the long run because both Fitzgerald and other members of his family participated in rebellions against the Crown and its interests. This included signing treaties with foreign powers that had an interest in taking Ireland away from the control of the English. One of these was the Pope, and another was Emperor Charles the V of the Holy Roman Empire. Both had vested interests in keeping the Irish population from being converted to Protestantism to the same degree the English population had since the start of Henry's reign. When the disloyalty became too severe, Henry executed several prominent members of the Fitzgerald family and instilled Edward Poynings (a capable soldier and administrator) to take over the Lordship of Ireland.

Edward had been integral in incorporating a new legal system wherein the legislation that was passed to control Ireland wasn't fully under Irish control. The legislation was created in England and the Irish parliament would then get to accept or reject it as it was (in other words, they weren't able to draw up their own legislation to handle the problems they faced). This created a legal system that was out of touch with the population that it was created to protect and control.

Another one of Edward's priorities to change

the legal system was the reduction of the number of monopolies on the island as they held too much power. This didn't only refer to the reduction of monopolies controlled by the Irish, but also those controlled by individuals loyal to England. Couple the reduction of monopolistic power with an increased number of military resources, and Ireland was gradually brought more under English rule.

Henry had seen the importance of ruling the island, thereby converting his title from "lord" of Ireland to "king" of Ireland, which no other English monarchs had done before him.

All these developments resulted in a lot more interference into the lives of the Gaelic and Gaelic-Norse lords than they'd been accustomed to over the previous two centuries. The lords already waged private wars between each other, but now the new English government was putting its fingers into these conflicts as well. An example of this is intervention into the inheritance matters of multiple lords and their successors, ultimately changing succession laws to male primogeniture. There were also instances of English soldiers and officials violating their mandate by killing lords and locals, as well as taking their land.

Many of the Gaelic and Gaelic-Norse lords

rose up against the newly rekindled English power. The king and his deputy didn't take kindly to this, with the result that lords who rose up had their lands confiscated for the benefit of the Crown. This practice continued during the reigns of Queen Mary and Queen Elizabeth I following Henry's death. Both these queens granted the use of the confiscated lands to people they had shipped from England to Ireland to make a more loyal population and workforce on the island. The people taken from England were mainly lower classed individuals and laborers who could make a useful labor force for those in charge of the new plantations that were created under the behest of the queens.

Another development that happened during the reigns of Queen Mary and Elizabeth was that martial law was implemented in many areas. The martial law allowed the English soldiers and people in power to execute individuals without the need for a trial by jury. The executions were largely carried out to reduce the amount of raiding by the locals. The Irish lords started getting fed up by the new rules being implemented because it prevented them from having private armies (in exchange for not needing to pay tax and getting their rental income entitlements formalized as statutes), forcing them to take responsibility for masterless men in their regions (to prevent those men from being executed), and they were being forced to do things in compliance with the ways of the English.

Insurrection was a result of this. The Pope declared Queen Elizabeth a heretic for her enforcement of Protestantism. He sent troops to assist the Irish in their attempt to overthrow the Crown's control of Ireland. The period of unrest lasted for the rest of the 16th century, with the most powerful Irish lord, Aodh Mór Ó Néil, forming a coalition with other Irish lords and getting the Spanish army involved in an attempt to oust the English. In the end, the English won and the Irish lords either accepted their lands back under strict rules or left the country in what's now called the Flight of the Earls in 1607.

The lands that had been confiscated were used as plantations and the English government invited many of its subjects to relocate to Ireland. The plantation that left the most lasting effect was the Plantation of Ulster in Northern Ireland. The plantation became home to many Scottish Presbyterians, English Protestants, and Welsh settlers, entrenching a firm cultural identity in the north of the island that's felt to the present day. This is one of the contributions to the political division between the present Republic of Ireland and Northern Ireland.

Along with the continued conflict between the Catholic and Protestant religious affiliations, there was also a cultural revolution that took place. The culture, laws, and language of the Irish were frowned upon by the new inhabitants of the island and the centralized government in Dublin, resulting in the government Anglicizing them. Thus, English common law and the legislation passed by the Irish Parliament (under the authority of the English government) became the law of the day. For all intents and purposes, the powerful lords of the Irish had been relegated to powerlessness by the removal of their hereditary rights, the incorporation of the English legal system, the influx of other ethnic groups that didn't accept the Irish lords' power, and the Protestant Ascendency.

The Protestant Ascendency refers to the gradual transition of power into the hands of Protestant elites and clergymen during the 17th century. This was particularly seen after the support of Irish Catholics for James II as he attempted to keep the Crown during the Glorious Revolution. After James was defeated in 1690, several steps were taken to give more power to the Protestants in Ireland and to limit the rights of the Catholics. One of these was that any individual who was Catholic would be kept from holding office; while another was that property and power would be kept out of the hands of the Catholic elites in accordance with the new penal law implemented by English powers.

The situation became difficult for many living in Ireland, especially when some of the steps taken by the English government affected the whole country, not just the Catholics—mainly trade policy discrimination. As a result, many emigrated from Ireland to other nations, especially the United States. This would continue for centuries as life remained difficult for many due to the laws being implemented by the English-backed Parliament in Ireland. Parliament would only gain independence in the late 18th century, by which time tens of thousands of people had abandoned the country.

The undesirable living conditions led both the Protestants and the Catholics to rise up against the English monarchy's presence in Ireland. They had been inspired by the developments of the French Revolution and the new democratic system of government that had been established there, along with the personal liberties that had been granted to the French as a result. The English government intervened swiftly in both the military and legal arenas, resulting in the abolition of the Irish Parliament and the acceptance of the English Parliament as the official lawmaking body for the entirety of the United Kingdom of Great Britain and Ireland. For all intents and purposes, the rebellion had failed, yet there were some freedoms granted to the Irish citizens as a result of the English government realizing its position was untenable if it kept on violating the personal dignities of Irish citizens.

The 19th century was marked by a lot of subsistence living due to the low amount of resources and trade opportunities allowed for the Irish population. Feudalism had taken hold over the preceding centuries and with the help of the new legal system that had been incorporated by the English government over the preceding century. Tenants would provide income from their harvests to the landlord in exchange for the land they lived on. And if they weren't able to provide income from harvests, then they would provide labor in exchange for lodging. The order of the day was small farms in most of the country outside of the largest towns and cities. The need to export much of the plant and animal output to keep their financial affairs afloat, much of the population had to rely on potatoes (and many a time only on potatoes) for food.

The Potato Famine of the 1840s (which resulted in the death of more than a million people) pushed the population's exodus from the island even further. About 2,000,000 Irish and Scottish settlers in Ireland fled for the United States and other countries. While abroad, those that managed to build up positions of prominence and financial success sent resources back to those in Ireland that were resisting English control. They also managed to get the support of prominent individuals in other nations towards Irish independence. The buildup of support contributed to the Fenian Movement of the 1860s, which was an unsuccessful revolution followed by a decade's-long resistance effort that eventually contributed to success in the 20th century.

Nationalism had been a hot topic for hundreds of years, but finally came to fruition in the early 1900s after the Easter Rising. The Easter Rising took place in 1916 when rebels occupied important buildings in London and put up resistance against the English military that was stationed there. When the rebellion had been subdued after a week (in which about 2,000 people were injured and killed), the English government executed the heads of the resistance. Their execution swayed public opinion in favor of the revolutionaries and their cause, with sustained unrest over the next 2 years.

In 1919, the Irish Republican Army started launching guerilla attacks against English forces all over the island. These were successful a lot of the time, necessitating the declaration of a ceasefire in 1921. The ceasefire was followed by the signing of a peace treaty by some of the Irish republican representatives, which stated that the violence would come to an end on the condition that the Irish were granted home-rule in all but 6 of the northern counties (although the independent counties would still remain a member of the British Commonwealth of Nations). While this was a step ahead, it wasn't good enough for other factions of the republican movement (especially the Irish Republican Army), thereby resulting in a civil war starting before the declaration of independence for the Irish Free State was even passed at the end of 1922.

In 1923, the Irish Free State's forces won against the Irish Republican Army, with the resultant end of the civil war. There was still some unrest, but this was majorly reduced. In 1937 a constitution was passed that emphasized the sovereignty of the new nation, which was to be renamed from the Irish Free State to Eire. Eire continued gradually unlinking itself with the UK, stating that it was a neutral party during the second world war. In 1949, true independence was gained when the Republic of Ireland Act was passed and all ties with the Commonwealth were severed—with Eire changing its name to the Republic of Ireland.

A further step that was taken to emphasize independence and enforce peace was to outlaw the Irish Republican Army in the Republic of Ireland, which was still fighting to make the six northern counties independent. All this managed to do, however, was to drive the Irish Republican Army underground, where it continued to do its work. In the 1970s, further violence built due to the tension between the Catholics and Protestants in Northern Ireland. The two Christian factions have yet to come to a real state of peace, with more than 3,000 people having died in the period of unrest that's existed since the 1970s.

Perhaps the most memorable and least peaceful incident of this violent period (also called the Troubles of Northern Ireland) was Bloody Sunday in 1972. There were protesters in Northern Ireland that wanted equal rights for the Catholic minority. There was inequality between the two factions on both a legal and an actual level. The British soldiers present open-fired on the protesters, killing 14 unarmed marchers in the process. This violation of human rights caught the attention of the world, resulting in negotiations that were held in the presence of neutral third parties (particularly the White House of the United States). The result was an agreement (signed in 1998) that reduced the amount of political and economic tension and determined a way forward for the nations.

Despite the violence of the Troubles and other recent historical events, the people of Ireland are still one nation. The pain and struggle in the nation's history is a shared experience by all on the island and is largely due to outside influences over the last few hundred years. The people of Ireland still have a strong unity in relation to the beliefs and mythology of the past, and this can be a binding foundation for growth towards one another in terms of acceptance. The next three chapters detail the mythology of Ireland for a good understanding of that foundation.

CHAPTER 5
Irish Paganism

Gaelic paganism was the religion of the ancient Irish people, particularly the Gaels. There were many deities and multiple forms of worship. Paganism refers to religious beliefs prior to Christianity, thus Gaelic paganism mainly refers to the religious beliefs held before the conversion of Ireland by Saint Patrick and the other early Irish saints. The Irish system of belief was so dear to the hearts and culture of its people that even when Christianity became the main religion of the island, many of the pagan practices formed a part of Irish Christianity. The main beliefs of Irish pagans were in a pantheon of deities, specifically the Tuatha Dé Danann, and the belief in the spiritual nature of all things, whether animate or inanimate.

Lebor Gabála

The Lebor Gabála, translated to the Book of Invasions, was written in the 12th century A.C.E. by scribes of the Christian church. It sought to integrate the Bible with the folklore and history of Ireland. It wrote of the multiple stages of human contact with Ireland and has come to be held as an authority on the cultural folklore of the nation.

The first human contact with Ireland was said to be one of Noah's granddaughters before the Great Flood. She had fled to the island with a group of just over 50 individuals when she was denied passage on the Ark. All the members of her party (including herself) died while protecting a man named Fintan from death. His survival during the flood was followed by him preserving himself by various transitions between animal forms and his human form until the next group of humans arrived on the island.

The next group was led by a great grandson of Noah named Partholan. This group came from a community that had been established after the flood. That community had broken out in widespread disease, so Partholan and his people fled in an attempt to keep alive. Upon their arrival to Ireland, all of them died within a week due to infection from the disease they'd carried with them.

Nemed, another descendant of Noah, came with the third group of people who were said to inhabit Ireland. The group (called the Nemedians) came from Scythia, which roughly equates to modern day Iran. While they journeyed to the island and upon their arrival they were attacked by the Fomorians. The Fomorians were sea pirates that were led by a king named Balor the Cyclop. The onslaught of the Fomorians proved to be too hostile for the Nemedians, leading them to flee the island and settle all over the known world.

Nobody inhabited Ireland over the next 200 years. The Fir Bolg were the first people to attempt habitation of the island after the 200-year period of desertion. They were the descendants of the Nemedians who had settled in Greece. Forts and homes were built as the Fir Bolg established themselves. They managed to create a thriving group until the arrival of the Tuatha Dé Dannan.

When the Tuatha Dé Dannan arrived, they first burned their ships. This meant that they wouldn't be able to return to their ancestral home and would be forced to make Ireland their new home. When they burned their ships, the whole of Ireland was covered in clouds and mist for three days and three nights. The sun couldn't get in, and all was difficult to see. Once the mists and clouds cleared, the Tuatha Dé Danann remained.

The Tuatha Dé Dannan were said to also descend from the Nemedians, albeit from Nemedians that had settled in northern Europe after being driven out of Ireland. The Tuatha Dé Danann had learned magic and, as such, were menacing foes for the Fir Bolg. The friction came to a head in the Battle of Moytura wherein the Tuatha Dé Danann emerged victorious. The Fir Bolg would go on to serve the Tuatha Dé Dannan following their defeat.

The story of how the Gaels and Gaelic got their names and how the Irish language came to be was also described in the Book of Invasions. It was said that one of Noah's descendants, Fenius, had been at the Tower of Babel. He had heard many languages and understood much of each. When he left, he chose Ireland as his destination. From all the best parts of the best languages he'd heard at the Tower, he created the Irish language.

One of Fenius' descendants, Goidil, gave his name to the language Fenius had created—

Gaelic. He also gave his name to the people who spoke it—the Gaels. Goidil's mom had the important role of founding Scotland. Her name was Scotta and she was the daughter of a Pharaoh. The similarity between her name and the name of Scotland is evident.

Another prominent member of Goidil's family was his grandson, Eber Scott. He was reputed to have conquered the whole of Spain, where he established himself as ruler. They were known as the Milesians while ruling the nation. Despite having a flourishing kingdom in Spain, the family didn't abandon Ireland. Eber Scott's son, Miledh, saw Ireland floating in the sky from one of the towers of his castle. He sent three of his sons, Meremon, Heber, and Ir, to Ireland where they in turn conquered the Tuatha Dé Danann. The Tuatha Dé Danann were driven into the Otherworld where they're said to still reside to this day.

Three of the Tuatha Dé Danann got the agreement of their conquerors that Ireland would be named after them in perpetuity. They were Erin, Banba, and Fodla—all daughters of the goddess Ernmas who was known as the mother goddess. The Milesians agreed to this and upheld the promise they gave. Eire is the local name for Ireland and means "plentiful land." To honor the other two sisters, both Banba (as the embodiment as the power of the land) and Fódhla (originally the name of the territories that included the Hill of Tara) are used as poetic and honorary names for the country.

With the Tuatha Dé Dannan subdued, the Milesians went on to form a powerful culture and civilization in Ireland.

Now that we've looked at the invasions that were presented as the history and part of the mythology of Ireland, we're going to take a deeper dive into its mythology.

The Four Mythological Cycles

There are four mythological cycles of importance in Gaelic paganism and mythology. These are the integral eras of stories and myths that define the Irish pre-Christian culture and that are still of importance when imparting Irish culture to this day.

The first is the mythological cycle. This covers the myths about when the Tuatha Dé Danann arrived in Ireland and the causes for them leaving Ireland for their underground homes in the sidhe. Further, the descendants (or in some cases, the altered manifestations) of the Tuatha Dé Danann, called the Aos Sí, are described largely in this cycle. The Aos Sí refers to the fairy and mythological creatures that are still celebrated in stories nationally and internationally to this day.

The second—the Ulster cycle—refers to the time around the first century A.C.E. It revolves around heroes of the time and the feats they accomplished. Most of the myths in this cycle take place in Ulster (the north of the island) and Leinster (the east of the island). These stories are tales of bravery and achievement, providing morals for listeners to live by.

The Fenian cycle is the third cycle. The most famous of all Irish heroes, Fionn mac Cumhaill, is the central point of this cycle, along with the other warriors that were a part of his team, the Fianna. The Fianna were the elite fighting force of the High King of Ireland, and they were the aspiration of many young men and women. This cycle provides tales of their most famous figures and their accomplishments over both human and mythological foes.

The fourth and final cycle is called the historical cycle. This part of Irish mythology describes the lives and interactions of the royals as told by court poets. As such, it is also often called the cycle of the kings. The kings, particularly the High King, held a lot of sway in ancient Irish society. Thus, this cycle provides a look into the personal lives of the most elite of the ancient Gaelic society.

The cycles were passed down from person to person and poet to poet using oral tradition. As was the style with the ancient Gaels, things weren't written down, rather favoring the sharp memories of the top poets of the land to keep the nation's memories and mythology alive. It was first written down (to our knowledge) in the 11th century A.C.E. by Christian monks who altered some of the material they were told to put it in a light that suits the Bible and Christian traditions more. That said, a lot can still be gleaned from those written works, despite alterations that were made to the stories they were told.

The Otherworld

The Otherworld is also called Mag Mell, which means "the plain of delights." It's hidden from the human world and consists of multiple locations. The sidhe is the first location, in which the faeries and mythical creatures of Irish lore reside. Life in the sidhe across Ireland is similar to human life, with fighting and power struggles being a part of daily life. Parts of the Otherworld similar to this can also be found in natural locations around Ireland, such as under lakes and in caves. Other parts of the

Otherworld are peaceful and paradisiacal—the islands beyond the west of Ireland.

If you wanted to get to one of the paradises, you would have to undertake difficult journeys full of feats of the body and mind. You couldn't just stumble upon these places, and if you got access, you would be able to stay for eternity. You could also go to one of these paradises if a deity or faerie invited you, normally for the purpose of teaching you something or because they were romantically interested in you. Sometimes you would end up in one of these paradises when you passed away and if you hadn't been reincarnated yet. Some of the most well-known paradise lands follow.

The Plain of Apples was an island that was the home of the Manannán mac Lir, the ocean and death god. His daughters lived there with him, and he raised his foster son Lugh there according to some accounts. It was one of the 150 Otherworld islands that were free of sickness, fighting, and lack of provision. The symbol of the island was a silver branch with golden apples on it. If you shook the branch, you could produce music that would induce relaxation, sleep, and healing.

The Isle of Joy, also called Moy Mael, was a land on which you would forget all your concerns. You wouldn't age while you were there, but if you left it, you would gain back many years, growing old or turning to dust if you stepped on other land—a few days on the island were equivalent to hundreds of years in the human world. While you were there, you would forget your life and the people in it, along with your cares and concerns. You would laugh heartily at most things, and you would be in a state of joy.

Another pleasant place without treachery or grief was the Land of Women. It was the home to many women and no men. A year there would translate to hundreds of years in the human realm, but you wouldn't notice as you didn't age on the island. The island was inhabited by beautiful women who would provide you with lodging, food, and comfort. You could stay there as long as you liked, and you didn't have to leave if you didn't want to.

The Land Beneath the Waves was a realm that was under the water. It consisted of orchards, grassy plains, and flowery meadows. It was inhabited by warriors and royal households. It was a place of peace and comfort that was shielded from the rest of the world. As with the other lands of Tír na nÓg, it was under the rule of Manannán mac Lir.

Tír na nÓg was the "Land of Youth," and was the home of the remaining Tuatha Dé Danann after they left the realms of Ireland. It was variously described as an island of the Otherworld, or as all of the Otherworld islands together. Manannán mac Lir was its ruler. With godly duties over the ocean and death, he was able to control his realm to have calm seas and to negate death for his inhabitants.

As a land free from want, and as somewhere that could only be entered upon by invitation, the Otherworld was a place for people of Ireland to strive to reach. It gave them motivation to be the best they could and to represent the ideals of behavior prescribed by the tales passed down to them.

The Wheel of the Year

The Wheel of the Year was, and still is, used to determine the phases of the seasons and the sun. The god Taranis was associated with the Wheel in that he was both the head of the gods in many Celtic religions, and he was the protector of the gods. As the head god, he wielded thunder and had control over storms and unpredictable weather. The association between weather changes and the passage of the year inevitably meant that he was linked with the cycle of the year as a whole. The Wheel was often used in depictions of him and symbolized more than just the passage of time, but also his strength and mobility as the protector of the other gods, and how fast a storm can catch you without you having expected it.

The Wheel of the Year consists of eight festivals at present. There were four during ancient times, but Neopagans have added four other festivals with ancient roots to the Wheel of the Year to mark some of the important changes during the year. For our purposes, we're going to examine all eight, with the ancient ones being referred to as the major ones and the more modern ones referred to as the minor ones. The four ancient ones were called the Imbolc, Beltane, Lughnasa, and Samhain. Due to the heavy reliance of the ancient Irish on the year's farming crops, these festivals were just as relevant to the food harvests as to the passage of time. The four more modern festivals are the Ostara, Litha, Mabon, and Yule.

Imbolc

The Imbolc is the first of the four major festivals in the year. The term can be given a literal translation of "in the Belly" due to it showing that spring is starting and winter's ending. In other words, it symbolizes the start of the agricultural year and the growth of the food that will later fill our bellies. The festival takes place on the first of February as the year transitions out of winter. During ancient times it was a momentous occasion because there was almost nothing to do and no way to get food during the winter months due to their harshness. Not only would plants start growing, but animal breeding would also commence for the year.

The festival was associated with the goddess Brigid. She was a goddess of the sun who was associated with motherhood, smithing, healing, poetry, cows and ewes (as life-giving motherly animals), cockerels (who signified the starting of the new day), and snakes (as a symbol of renewal). Her name is translated to "exalted" or "powerful," which closely relates to her ability to generate growth with the rays of the sun, and to inspire with the inner healing and vitality she can bring about in all of us. A common theme in the stories about Brigid throughout the various Celtic cultures that worshiped her is that she is to be seen as an embodiment of fire and all the qualities related to it (whether it be light, heat, inspiration, punishment and justice, or otherwise).

Fire is an integral part of the festival. Bonfires are lit and kept going throughout the festival as they invite the sun back after a long winter of cold and shorter days. It's a time of jubilation that symbolizes rebirth and purification. People use well-water to purify themselves for the start of the new agricultural year. While maidens and young men used to meet for ritual mating in ancient times to mark this period of renewed fertility in the year. In essence, this festival is about the coming of new life after the lifeless period of winter.

Beltane

This festival is celebrated at the start of the summer when the weather warms up. It's held on the first of May, resulting in its alternative name, May Day. As with Imbolc, it's also linked with fertility—due to plants becoming greener and growing stronger. Another name for Beltane is the Fire Festival as the translation of the word Beltane is "bright fire." As with the Imbolc, fire is seen as a cleansing element that purifies and heals. To celebrate this aspect of the festival's significance, bonfires are lit for people to sing, dance, eat, and generally be merry around. Like in prehistoric times, the central fires are seen as a way for people to come together and be protected while remaining social with one another.

This festival is one of the more popular times

for people to get married because of the fertility connotation with the festival and time period. In fact, it was believed that this festival marked when the gods and goddesses of the Celtic pantheon got married to one another. A superstition that developed over the years was to jump over a broomstick to mark transitions into a new life as a married couple. The couple also needed to wear a special wedding ring, called a claddagh ring, which signified their union.

Lughnasa

Lughnasa usually takes place on the first of August each year, marking the start of the year's harvest season. To commemorate the occasion, it was common for participants to make corn dollies with the final sheaf of grain of the harvest. It's a time of abundance like no other in the year, and as such is a period when much celebration takes place. There are typically many stalls piled with the harvest of the year, along with foodstuffs that have been prepared for the occasion. One of the more interactive activities of the festival is when young men and women forage for bilberries to make bilberry cake with. Bilberries are a traditional sign of affection and are thus used in matchmaking gifts.

The festival is held in honor of the god Lugh and was believed to represent the time when he returned as a grown man to Ireland from the Tír na nÓg (the land of paradise and youth). He had been taken there as a baby and grew up under the guidance of his foster father. When his foster father saw that the Tuatha Dé Danann were in trouble, he knew that he needed to take Lugh back to bring him to their aid. Before he did this, however, he gave Lugh the Fragarach, a sword that could compel others to tell the truth. Upon his return, Lugh was able to help inspire the Tuatha Dé Danann to overcome the Fomorians in battle.

In association with the festival, Lugh dedicated the Tailteann Games to be held in honor of his foster mother (Tailtiu) each year. They were held from approximately 1600 B.C.E. to 1171 A.C.E. The games were a hub of interaction, with people participating in sport, trade, dating, and feasts.

Samhain
Samhain is the last of the four major festivals during the year. This is the festival that marks the official end of the harvest period. It takes place from the 31st of October to the 1st of November. The festival was perhaps the most important of the four major ones and was

participated in by all citizens during ancient times. It would last three days and three nights (or in some cases, six days) in early periods, with all members of a king or chief's population needing to present themselves as present to the leader. It was believed that you would be cursed if you didn't present yourself.

As with the other major festivals, fire was a key component of the festivities. First, a druid would light a community fire. Community members would then light torches to take home and light their own hearths with the fire the druid had lit initially. This was partly because it was thought that the barrier to the Otherworld thinned at this time of the year, so the fire would keep you and your family safe. Dressing up as monsters or animals was another approach taken to keep inhabitants from the Otherworld from kidnapping you or your children. That said, not all spiritual and fantastical matters were believed to pose danger to participants of the festival. The ancestors of members of the community were believed to visit their families during the festival, allowing the families to update them about the year's events and for the children to play games with their ancestors.

Sacrifices and offerings were also important when participating in this festival so that spirits and creatures from the Otherworld wouldn't curse you or your community. Safety and security were a priority at Samhain. When the festival commenced, commanders and soldiers sat on thrones that had been prepared for the occasion. Further, it wasn't uncommon for the death penalty to be doled out for any civil disobedience that had taken place during the festivities. Cattle were sacrificed, and offerings were made in the form of food, drink, or smaller sacrifices. That said, the food and drink wasn't all for the purpose of offerings; in fact, it was common for all the days of the festival to be rife with feasting and drinking alcohol to excess.

Samhain was absorbed into Christian festivities due to its popularity. Later in time it came to be known as All Souls's Day, then All Hallow's Eve, and finally as Halloween—the popular holiday we celebrate annually today. The trick-or-treating we see today is a spin-off of some of the aspects of the celebration from earlier times.

Ostara

This festival takes place on the spring equinox in April of each year. It serves to symbolize the middle of spring, which is why it was named after the spring goddess, Eostre. Due to the connotation of spring with fertility and growth, the symbols of the hare and the egg are synonymous with this festival. Both of these are symbols related to the Eostre and had connotations with growth. A hare was believed to die each night and get reborn in the morning when it emerged from its burrow, hence the connection with the idea of rebirth and growth.

Eggs were similarly seen as sources of rebirth and growth, with the added nuance that the yolk and egg white were seen as an example of the symmetry of the world (with the yolk being the sun and the white being the sky). The balance of the egg also ties in with the balance of the equinox due to the day and the night being of equal length. The legend behind the festival is that Eostre found a frozen bird while wandering and took pity on it. She gave it life by turning it into a hare, but the hare retained the ability to lay eggs. This myth gave further credence to the concept of renewal associated with both the hare and the egg.

This festival is newer than the four original ones in that it was first celebrated starting in the eighth century A.C.E. It was a festival that was a combination of Christian, Celtic, and Germanic traditions revolving around spring, fertility, and planting of crops. Birds and flowers are both symbolic of the celebration in that birds are the signal for a new day and the return of the sun, while flowers bring to mind the idea of fertility. Easter possibly got its name from this festival and the goddess associated with it, considering the similarity between the terms Eostre and Easter.

Litha

Litha is an important festival that celebrates the middle of the summer, also known as the summer solstice (the longest day of the year). As such, it's a day that's commonly spent outdoors appreciating the daylight that's representative of the mythological Oak King—a deity of daylight. On this day, you celebrate the inner strength and light you have, often meditating if you practice Neopaganism. The light of the day is commonly celebrated with a fire, whether it be a large bonfire or a small fire you make in a pot at home.

The ancients (both of Celtic and other cultures) celebrated this day with various traditions. The Celts in particular held bonfires where people could dance and enjoy themselves. If they were brave enough, they could jump through the bonfire for good luck. It was also a good time to get married or to build on the fire of your romantic life by practicing love magic— or at least, that's what's practiced by many

Neopagans today.

The key myth underlying this holiday was the triumph of the Holly King over the Oak King. The Oak King represented daylight, whereas the Holly King represented the night, thus the lengthening of the nights after the summer solstice. This would be rebalanced after Yule when the Oak King won out against the Holly King, resulting in the increased length of the day between the winter and summer solstices.

Mabon

Mabon takes place on the fall equinox, near the end of September. It's to acknowledge the dark times to come in the winter ahead, and to emphasize balance in life. It takes place after much of the year's difficult farming and harvest work was completed, thus allowing families to put up their feet and enjoy the fruits of their labors. The day is marked by completing tasks that have been left unfinished, cleaning out the house, and to get rid of things that you don't need in the house. This allows you to enjoy the period more so that you can reflect on the things you've accomplished in the year and reward yourself with some leisure.

The festival was often three days long, which was the period of the abduction of the god who the festival was named after. Mabon was a sun god who was the son of the Great Goddess of the Earth. When he was newly born, he was stolen for three days, in which time the world went dark. There's an undercurrent of understanding that winter is coming soon after the festival and that we need to be thankful for the sun and the light as it's contributed to our lives over the period leading up to the harvest.

Some of the celebrations involved pouring of libations on the trees of the forest. This was to pay homage to the Green Man, who was the god of the forest in some Celtic cultures. Other offerings made to him included fertilizer, wine, ciders, and herbs. In general, the festival was a period of giving thanks and appreciating what you've been given and what you've worked for.

Yule

Yule happens in the middle of winter, from the 20th to the 23rd of December (which is why some call it midwinter). It's a celebration that takes place on the winter solstice when the day is the shortest of any in the year, and the night is the longest. It's steeped in mythology, with the belief that the Oak King beats the Holly King on this day, thereby allowing the days to get longer for the rest of the year. As such, it's a period of hope and revitalization of the world.

The rebirth of light is an underlying concept

to the celebration. In some Celtic tribes it was believed that the God of Light or the Sun Child is given birth in the interval of the festival. To celebrate the return of light and the sun, bonfires are held at home and in public places. Bonfires have different significance during different festivals—in this festival it's a way of welcoming the increase of sunlight back. It's also a time of community and family spirit, with people drinking and feasting for the whole night.

The eight festivals above are important aspects of the Gaelic Pagan religions. They were a way for communities to come together and to provide them with hope and purpose throughout the four seasons of the year.

In the next chapter we're going to explore another central theme of Gaelic Paganism—mythological creatures and figures.

CHAPTER 6
Mythological Creatures

Mythological creatures are an important part of most cultures around the world. No more so than the Irish, with an influence from the Gaels and other prehistoric people. Due to the metropolitan nature of the Irish over the last few millennia, many of the mythological creatures have been introduced from other cultures or have been exported to other cultures. As such, we are familiar with them on an international pop culture level (such as mermaids), albeit in a glamorized form. This chapter will delve into the creatures that make Irish mythology tick.

The Aos Sí

The Aos Sí are also known as the sidhe. They are the faerie creatures that the modern Irish sometimes refer to as "the folk," "the good neighbors," or "the gentry." They are said to live in the thousands of earthen mounds scattered around Ireland, which is why the term "sidhe," translated to "the people of the mounds," was chosen to describe them. There are two main beliefs about how they came to be. The one is that they are the Tuatha Dé Danann who settled underground in the Otherworld after they were defeated by the Milesians. The other belief is that the Aos Sí are their descendants and have gradually changed shape and size over the millennia. What is generally agreed upon is that there are many types of Aos Sí, and that they have different abilities and dispositions towards humans.

Faeries

Faeries aren't the stereotypical fairy that we see in Disney movies and series. While they serve as the inspiration for those portrayals, there are actually many types of faeries. Some are beautiful and elvish in nature, while others are akin to hags. They are more often than not believed to be smaller than the average human and they are almost always attributed with magical abilities. They don't normally have wings (although some do), but many of them can fly or travel at high speeds.

The life of a faerie can be quite pleasant. They enjoy their time in the Otherworld by singing, dancing, feasting, playing games, making love, and fighting. The lives of high-born faeries are very comfortable, and they have power over many lower-born faeries in their sidhe. But even the lowest-born of the faeries are powerful. They sometimes use it for malicious purposes, in which case it's called black magic, but it's normally used for helpful or naughty reasons. They love playing annoying tricks on humans, which is why some of us are thought of as having bad luck. There are also many that enjoy helping humans, in which case you may believe you have good luck.

Leprechauns

Leprechauns are popularly shown as very small older men with green clothes and a hat. They're often described as having a short fuse and being a bit too fond of the bottle. Leprechauns are known for being capable cobblers and being very good with money. The history of the leprechaun is that they're descended from the luchorpán (water sprites) of the eighth century A.C.E. These water sprites mated with household faeries that stole into cellars and drank all your alcohol at night. Their offspring were the leprechauns who kept the mischievous ways of their ancestors.

They're so fond of money that they might just trick you out of yours. When you make a deal with a leprechaun, the silver they give you from their pouch will likely return to it once the transaction is completed; and gold they give you from the pouch will turn to leaves or to ashes. What's more is they likely won't feel guilt for tricking you out of your money because most leprechauns see humans as silly creatures that are too greedy for their own good. Despite their tricky behavior and fondness of money, they aren't fond of get-rich-quick schemes. Leprechauns work to make their money and don't have a problem with putting in effort. They will trick you to teach you to think in the same way.

In other words, while they are mischievous, it's with the purpose of making you comfortable with the idea of working hard and not taking the quick route to wealth. That said, you might still be in luck to get rich quick if you catch one or get ahold of their magical token (usually their enchanted ring or an enchanted amulet). They'll either give you their treasure or they'll grant you three wishes in order to buy their freedom. So, if you're in for the chase, the telltale sign of a leprechaun being in your vicinity is the tap-tap-tapping sound of their small hammer while they're making shoes.

Clurichaun

The Clurichaun is a type of leprechaun, but with a whole extra level of mischievousness. They look similar, with small bodies and an old male appearance. But they're a bit more on the rough side, taking chances to steal and borrow wherever they go. If one asks you for money, don't be surprised if you end up with nothing; the same goes for a business agreement or a trade.

Their mischief extends beyond monetary matters. They love breaking into houses and stealing from your cellar—much like their ancestors did. If you have pets or livestock, they might just steal them too. Clurichaun have been spotted riding dogs, goats, fowl, and sheep across the countryside. So, don't fall into the trap of offering one a place to stay for the night or letting them watch your pets while you're getting something—you might just end up never being able to find them again.

Far Darrig

These are a type of leprechaun of a very disheveled and dirty appearance. There's one type, called rat boys, that have an appearance almost like a humanoid rat. They have a long snout, a skinny tail, skin that's dark and hairy, and a staff of blackthorn wood and a human skull as a topper. They tend to be sociable and like to hang around with humans. You'll find them around rivers, under bridges, close to sewers, in landfills, or on the coast. They often enter people's homes without invitation, taking advantage of their hospitality by lighting a fire and sponging off of your food, drink, and tobacco or cigarettes. The conversation will flow freely and engage you but will be full of contradictions. The rat boys are also fond of playing pranks on you, albeit lighthearted ones that don't lead to real harm.

Another type of far darrig, the red men, are more malicious. It's not so much that they wish to do harm, but their addiction to gnarly mischief leads to inevitable damage. Their favorite pastime is to kidnap people (adults and babies) and to plot different traps to kidnap people. If they capture a child, they'll swap it with a changeling to bring bad luck to your household. If you're an adult, they'll lock you up in a dark room in their house and spook you by letting out their evil-sounding cackle outside in their lair. You'll only be let out on the odd occasion when they want you to make them a meal of skewered hag, after which you'll be taken back to the dark room. Eventually they'll let you free so that you can return home, but not until after they've sufficiently demoralized you.

The red cap is a slight variation from the red men. They are normally found in old forts or churches, especially when these are abandoned. The sound of barley being ground against stone is characteristic of them, and if this becomes louder or longer to an excessive extent, then it's an omen of death. The red cap has no problem with committing murder when you enter their home, using either stones that it throws at you or its trusty pike. If it manages to kill you, it'll use your blood to keep its cap's dye bright—with their life force being strengthened when the cap is brighter and saturated with fresh blood. The red cap is recognized by its stature as a stocky and short old man with long teeth, fingers and nails, iron boots, and red eyes. The way to vanquish them is to recite Christian scripture in their presence, in which case they'll vanish and leave behind one of their teeth.

Pooka

This is a type of goblin that can cause a lot of problems in your daily life. It's a shapeshifter, so you might spot it in any number of forms. The major forms are as a rabbit, goat, dog, bull, donkey, or horse—with a horse being the main form. If you see it in horse form, it will likely have a penchant for trampling all over your garden or crops. Humanoid forms include young men or beautiful women. But, in all of the forms, it'll likely have red or golden eyes that betray its faerie nature.

In all its forms, it might try to do annoying things to get a kick out of you. This includes mild annoyances such as stealing the vegetables you've grown to violent and dangerous things such as causing buildings to collapse. There have also been stories of pookas being in a particularly foul temperament, leading them to sink ships with their crews. But this is a severe case and most pookas wouldn't sink to that level. In fact, some are downright well-intentioned, with it being willing to provide you with advice on problems you're facing.

An average pooka, however, is neither highly evil nor kind-hearted. They're in an unpleasant middle ground of enjoying playing with our lives as if we're toys for their enjoyment. A favorite pastime is for them to call your name so that you come outside your home to meet them. If you come outside, they'll kidnap you; while if you stay inside, they'll damage your home and land. If they kidnap you, don't freak out too much because they'll likely give you a wild ride that leaves you disoriented and forgetful of the experience. This is especially true if you're drunk and on your way back home after a night out.

Banshee

A banshee is a female figure who is often described as beautiful, but with red eyes from crying. She dons a green dress and gray coat. When she senses your death or the death of someone in your family is coming, she'll cry in your vicinity. It's a heart-wrenching tune that'll fill you with grief, although in many cases the crying is overwhelming and leads to your ears hurting. It's been said by many that if you manage to catch a banshee, she'll tell you how you're going to die. So, if you think you're ready to find out about your death, a banshee is your best bet.

One of the best-known tales of a banshee was one in which the banshee wasn't a harbinger of death, but a woman in love. She had appeared to Connla the Fair and told him that she was of the sidhe and all who resided there lived eternally without need or conflict. The realm of which she spoke was the Otherworld (also known as Mag Mell), and she intended for him to come with her and be happy there. His father, Conn the

Hundred-Fighter, heard her and called his druid to intervene by preventing her voice from being heard.

She threw an apple to nourish Conn while she was away so that he would be sustained without her presence. The apple was all he could eat and all he wanted to eat for the month following her disappearance—a self-replenishing apple. She returned after the month with the druid's spell worn-off, thus being audible to all. She warned Connla against using the services of his druid again and she reiterated the pleasures waiting for Conn if he came with her. Conn took a leap of faith into her crystal boat, and they sailed away—a journey to the Otherworld.

Dullahan

The dullahan is likely one of the scariest creatures anywhere. It's a headless horseman that carries a human spine as a whip and his head under his arm as a lantern. The head glows allowing him to cast his fearful light around for people to see. The horse he sits on is always a black stallion—sometimes headless too. If you see the dullahan, then you know that someone is going to die where he stops. Unlike the banshee who warns that someone is going to die, the dullahan brings death with him like a cloak to the unsuspecting individual when he arrives. If you see the dullahan, just hope that he doesn't stop in front of you…or that you won't die of fright.

Leanan Sídhe

These are sometimes also called a faerie sweetheart. If it's a woman, it will be an attractive and enticing individual; while if it's a man, it'll be handsome, but vampiric in appearance. They're slightly elvish when you look at them, but in an enticing way. The Leanan sídhe are fairies that provide you with a burning passion that can inspire you and bring success into your life, so long as you make them happy in the bedroom. If you displease them, however, don't be surprised if you wind up dead soon after—they don't take well to offense. So, it's up to you whether you allow one into your life, but just know that as much as they can bring you to greater heights than you might have expected, they can take away all you have just as fast.

Changelings

If you have a newborn, it's important to watch out for changelings. These are the deformed or mentally incapacitated offspring of faeries that they swap out for human children. The human child will be raised as if they were a faerie and will likely be unaware of their real parents' existence. Likewise, the changeling will now be raised by you and will, for all intents and purposes, your child. There were initially believed to be two ways to get rid of a changeling and get your child back. The first was to torture it, and the second was to get it to laugh.

The first method was cruel and resulted in many cases of scarring child abuse in parents who had mistakenly thought their child was a changeling. Many people didn't realize that a changeling is incapable of doing anything other than singing or making music, hence someone who only has a form of disability is certainly not a changeling. It's not only cruel and illegal to do this, but ineffective. The other method works far better because even if the child isn't a changeling, you'll have made their day better by making them laugh.

Similar to a changeling, you occasionally find a stock, whose an adult that's been swapped out for a wooden carving that looks and acts like a human. At first it will sound and act well, but soon it will become bedridden and absent-minded. Finally, it will start dying, resulting in the smell of decomposing wood and a wooden skin texture and color. Meanwhile, the human is in the Otherworld—either under their own choice or from being taken as a slave or worker.

Fachan

Also called Peg Leg Jack, this a giant-like creature that has caused many deaths by scaring the observer out of their wits. In addition to a fondness for attacking humans unawares (with a mace), their appearance is such an assault on your senses that you can't help but be frightened beyond belief. They have a giant-like size, a tuft or mane of hard hair or black feathers, one eye, a warped arm coming out of their chest, and a single leg. Their leg has an immense amount of strength allowing them to bound with great speeds and letting them appear seemingly out of nowhere, which only contributes to the alarm you get when you see them.

Cú Sidhe

These are also known as hounds of rage. They're large, black or dark green dogs that hunt for the faeries. They might kidnap human women and they lead people that have passed on to the afterlife. Further, they nurse faerie babies, thus providing them with strength. It's considered an omen of death if you see one, almost like the association between the Grim and death in Harry Potter and the Prisoner of Azkaban. Tell-tale signs that differ it from other large, black dogs are its fiery eyes (sometimes one normal and one fiery one), its size (the size of a small horse), and its brutish nature. In some cases, they're snow white with one red eye and one red ear. You're not likely to find them far from bogs, moors, earthen mounds, or rocky outcrops.

Cait Sí

The cait sí is a cat of the sidhe that's larger than normal and of ghostly appearance. They have black fur and a white patch on their chest. The cat is actually a witch that has the ability to transfigure, although she might still walk on two legs when in cat form if she knows nobody is watching. She can't transfigure back and forth more than nine times, which is potentially where the phrase "a cat has nine lives" originated. Although they're more common in Scotland than Ireland, they can still be found in the Green Isle. The reason to guard against them is that they like to steal away the souls of the dead, thus denying them peace. If you need to protect against this, know that they'll avoid cold—hence them almost never entering morgues.

Wyrm

A wyrm is a reptilian worm of great size. It's the Irish form of a dragon, albeit without wings and only rarely with fire-breathing abilities. In some cases, they might have clawed feet, but this isn't a given. Wyrms like to rest at the bottom of water bodies, in caves, or in swamps. When they occupy a marsh or swamp, you'll notice there's a slight tinge of disease in the air. This is because they're toxic creatures that poison their environments—with their blood being especially toxic.

The creatures are extremely powerful and have been included in many of Ireland's greatest myths. They are so powerful that when a hero tries to overpower one, they might create lakes and rivers in their wake while getting away. The most impressive wyrm was likely Caoránach, the mother of all demons and wyrms—the epitome of evil. She was so powerful that it was said Saint Patrick himself had to slay her.

Saint Patrick was also said to have gotten rid of Ollipheist, another legendary wyrm of Ireland who wasn't known to be violent. The wyrm had heard that the saint was on a journey to vanquish him, so he became angrier and angrier. He grew so angry that he gobbled up a bagpipe player that was passing by. The piper, however, was drunk and didn't even notice he'd been swallowed up, so he kept on playing. This nauseated Ollipheist to the extent that he vomited up the piper, and fearing for the danger of the approaching saint, he fled the island. In the process, he created Ireland's greatest river—

the Shannon.

Demna Aeoir

Also called demons of the air, these are flocking creatures that roam the skies. They have wicked intentions and drag people to hell, whether it be from funerals or the battlefield. Their demonic shape is somewhat similar to that of spectral black birds. They are believed to be the cause of much of the stormy weather that keeps us up at night. Their shrieks crescendo into the loud, awful sound of the wind in the worst storms. They'll flock through the air, moving like schools of fish move through the ocean.

Sluagh

The sluagh are somewhat similar to the demna aeoir in that they also have the appearance of shadow-like black birds. Further, they also travel in great numbers that form writing clouds of dark smoke. Individual sluagh are found to have gnarly taloned hands and feet and they have a slightly humanoid form, but with a darkened gray skin and beaklike face. These creatures have the cruel desire of taking people who have found love and getting them to do heinous acts that can't be forgiven (such as maiming and killing people). In the process, they snatch up the soul of the now-damned person and have their nasty way with it, but only after abusing the person by dragging their body through the mud and pools until the body can't stand it any longer.

Fear Gorta

The fear gorta is also known as the hungry man. He's an emaciated figure that shows up with a begging bowl and dirty appearance. He looks like he's on the verge of death from starvation and he'll have a green tinge to his skin. If you provide him with nourishment or good hospitality of some nature, he'll bless you with good luck. But, if you mock him, scorn him, or otherwise mistreat him, he'll punish you with an unending hunger. No matter how much you eat, you'll remain hungry—from now until the day you die. He'll also bring you illness and bad luck to compound the trouble you'll face from hunger.

The power of the fear gorta is such that he can make you a wealthy ruler if you're a poor person; and he will make you into a vagabond if you treat him badly, even if you're a business magnate. The nature of a fear gorta is embedded in his creation. If a person dies of starvation next to a sidhe, this is their fate—they will be a bringer of disease, famine, and gloom.

Alp Lauchra

This is a newt-like parasite that can make your life a living hell. Also called a joint eater or just halver, this creature is a lover of food, especially good food. You get this parasite by spending time in streams or rivers where there's a lot of green life in the water (i.e. algae, spores, seeds, and microbes, among others). You might not notice it's entered your body, but if it has it will sit comfortably in your belly while you slowly degenerate. It eats everything you eat, especially the tastiest bits of the good or the parts of the food that contain the most nutrition.

You'll start getting ill from the lack of nutrition flowing into your body, requiring you to take drastic action to get rid of the hunger and to start building up your body's food reserves again. The easiest method is to eat a lot of salty beef and to not drink any water, resulting in you feeling parched. Don't drink water at this stage, but lay down next to a stream or other body of water with your mouth open. The creature will eventually scramble out of your mouth so that it can rehydrate, at which point you should make sure to close your mouth and to avoid touching it. If you do happen to touch it with your skin, you'll end up with a numbness in the part of your body where you came into contact with it.

The second option is to get someone to sit on your belly, while another person dangles a tasty morsel above your mouth. Eventually the hunger and the temptation will become too much for the alp lauchra, leading it to abandon the safety of your belly to try and snatch up the food. At this point you need to close your mouth and move fast to get away from the creature, so it doesn't re-enter your body.

Hags

Hags were old women who looked weak but were actually strong. The mother of all the other gods and goddesses was a hag, which shows the amount of power that could be wielded and imparted by one of these beings. Hags were known to be wise and to have magical control of the elements and the weather. If they were angry, they could create storms, and when they walked the lands, they made them barren. They had a nasty sense of humor, often sitting on people's chests at night to give them nightmares, and then putting the person into a state of sleep paralysis if they woke up in the middle of the nightmare. The person would be unable to move until the morning, no matter their level of discomfort or fear.

The Storm Hag

She is often called the Cailleach or the Queen

of the Winter. Her strength thrives in winter, particularly nearer the end when the days start getting longer again. She holds a lot of power in her hands of blue-green fire. Not a particularly beautiful hag, she's described as ogreish, tall, and warped with a glowing face. Her main influence on human life is when she generates great storms that wipe out ships, towns, and crops. In the ocean water, she is known to have the ability to create waves that tower dozens of feet high.

Water Horse

You might have heard of a film with this name, although the creature isn't exactly the same as in the film. The water horse is, in fact, a long creature with the tail of a whale, the body and head of a horse, short and stumpy legs with large feet or large fins in the place of legs. A water horse is covered in a black hide and has a flowing mane on its neck. When you look into their eyes, there's a distinctive glint that shines back at you. They are bothersome creatures that will eat your animals and your crops. They might even have an evil nature on occasion where they trick passers-by to approach while they're in the shallows, only to put the traveler on their back and pull them down to a watery death.

Man-Wolves of Ossory

The Kingdom of Ossory was situated in the southeastern part of Ireland from around the first to the 11th centuries A.C.E. Although it was a part of Leinster, it remained independently controlled for much of its existence.

It was believed there were people in Ossory who could transform into wolves, with the body, temperament, and appetite of a wild wolf while in the transformed state; although you wouldn't develop an appetite for human flesh, no matter how long you were in the form. If they elected to change into wolf form, they would have to leave their human body behind at home, which could be problematic. Your body looked dead while you were in wolf form, and if someone chose to remove it, you wouldn't be able to change back into human form. Thus, it was best practice for friends to be warned when you were going to change into your wolf form, otherwise you might have to stay in the form forevermore.

Another nuance of the transformation was that you would transfer any physical changes to your human body that you had experienced while being a wolf. An example of this would be if you had a large meal and you got covered in blood—your human form would be covered in blood when you returned to it later on. Another example was if you were stabbed by a farmer as a wolf, in which case your human body would have a stab wound that needs medical attention when you re-transfigure.

Dwarves

The dwarves of Ireland aren't the benign little creatures we know from Snow White. They're small creatures that are related to water sprites, much like leprechauns are. The realm of the dwarves is in the Otherworld, under the lakes and seas of this world. They're group creatures, much like those in the Lord of the Rings franchise, albeit less stoic and severe. Further, they're not obsessive on the matters of treasure and making shoes...at least not in the Irish strains of dwarves. Rather, they live similar to humans under lords and kings who command and protect them while they carry on with lives much like ours.

Abhartach

The abhartach is a type of vampire that once plagued the Irish countryside. He was originally a chief that had a penchant for commanding his people in a way that was much like a dictator. His people wanted to be treated better, so they beseeched another chief to come and slay him, which the other chief did. What nobody expected was that he climbed back out of his grave with a taste for human blood. He demanded a bowl of fresh blood for his consumption from the villagers, so the chief who had killed him originally came to the villagers's salvation once more.

Once more, the abhartach got up from his grave with a desire for blood, so the chief who killed him consulted the druid for advice. The druid told him to bury the abhartach upside down and to lay a stone upon the grave after killing him with a wooden sword. This was done, and finally the villagers were free from his tyranny. The abhartach is thus a vampiric dwarf whose grave should not be disturbed, lest you want to release his evil upon the Irish countryside once more.

Dearg Due

The dearg due is another vampire of Irish origin. She was created through neglect and loneliness. Originally a beautiful woman from Waterford, she was married off to a chief that soon showed he had no interest in her at all. He neglected giving her attention and she soon got so lonely that she left the castle to go die by herself. Upon her death she was resurrected as an undead version of herself with a taste for revenge. She found the chief who had rejected her so severely and she unleashed her wrath upon him. Once she was done, however, she had grown fond of the taste for blood, leading her to become a vampiric undead shell of herself.

The Questing Beast

This creature's mother was a princess who lusted after her own brother. She made a deal with a demon that she would have sex with him if he made the brother fall in love with her. When she slept with the demon, she was impregnated, and she blamed the pregnancy on her brother. The king, her father, had her brother sentenced to death by having a pack of dogs tear him up as punishment for the crime she falsely accused him of. He cursed her before his death by saying she would give birth to a demon who made the same sound as a pack of dogs.

She later gave birth to such a demon—a demon with the head and neck of a snake, the body of a leopard, the thighs of a lion, and the feet of a male deer. In other renditions of the story, the creature was small, soft, and beautiful. Whichever rendition you accept, the creature made the frightful sound of a pack of dogs, either by itself, or by the offspring in its belly that were clamoring to get out. Eventually, the questing beast gave birth to its children, who then promptly tore her up as her uncle had been.

Selkie

These were creatures that could transform between the shape of a seal and human, although preferring the shape of a seal. They had a skin for each form, and if you were to get ahold of their seal skin, you would be able to entrap them. They would live normal human lives in this case, but always looking for their skin and seeking their life in the waves, even when they had full human families. If they found the skin, they would run away and resume their life as a seal, only returning once every year to see their children.

Female selkies were beautiful women in human form, and male ones came in the form of handsome men. The male selkies would use their good looks to seduce human women, having a particular taste for dissatisfied women, especially those whose husbands had been away for long. Some claim that selkies were condemned souls who had been punished with the life of a seal for their actions.

Merrow

The merrow was an Irish mermaid, creatures that were much less glamorous than what we see now in films and series. The females were beautiful women who were irresistible when they brushed their hair. They swam with the tail of a fish, but could come onto land if they put on a special cap. She would come on land to take human lovers, but if one of those lovers took her cap, they could force her to remain in human form while they had their way with her. If she wasn't trapped, however, she would bring her lovers back to the water with her, where she would kill them and trap their souls.

Male merrow were frightful looking creatures who the females refused to mate with. They had green hair and scales, and their arms were stubby. The refusal of female merrows to mate with them because they preferred to mate with human men made many male merrows hate sailors and capture them from their ships or the water. The men who were captured would have their souls imprisoned beneath the water, preventing them from escape and peace.

Dobhar Chú

This was a monster that inhabited lakes, rivers, or the sea. Its name was translated to "the hound of the deep," and it looked like an otter with flippers. They were large at seven feet long, and their flippers were often bright orange. These creatures were said to be the children of the Loch Ness monster in Scotland but had traveled to Ireland to exact revenge on its population because of Saint Columba rescuing a man from the Loch Ness monster. They had a taste for humans and would exact their bloodthirsty desires without a moment's hesitation. Their shape and size allowed them to travel vast distances quickly, with some reported sightings as far away as North America.

Ellén Trechend

This was a giant three-headed vulture-like bird who could breathe fire. It appeared from a cave along with goblins and copper-colored birds to cause devastation to Ireland. With the help of the birds and goblins, it was able to do exactly that, ruining the lives of many people in the process. Its reign of terror could only be ended once the poet warrior, Amergin, killed it to bring order back to Ireland.

Ghille Dhu

You're very unlikely to ever see a ghille dhu as they're known for being secretive to the point of paranoia when it comes to human presence. They're almost solely found in the forest, so you're very unlikely to find them in or around human settlements. If you're in the forest and they feel like you might be looking at them, they might just get the forest's undergrowth to grow around your limbs and bind you in place so that they have enough time to flee. It might be very difficult to get out of the foliage they've grown around you, so be prepared when you go into the woods so that you're safe in the case of a survival situation. In contrast, the ghille dhu is much more comfortable with children than adults, leading them to ensure children find their way safely out of the undergrowth if they get lost in the forest.

Féár Fortach

This was a type of hungry patch of land near a Sidhe that was covered by grass. It would be created when vile acts took place around the holy areas around the Sidhe. When stepped on, the grass would impart an unending hunger that you could never satiate. If you ate what would have been your fill at every meal thereafter, you would still starve to death, or at the very least turn into a physical husk. The only way to protect against these patches was to put a crust of bread in your pocket or to scatter oat bread crumbs on it. Alternatively, you could scatter salt on the patch and burn it.

This chapter included many of the creatures you may have encountered in Irish mythology. They ranged from the benign and beautiful to the ugly and vengeful. In the next chapter we will explore figures that were integral to the nation's mythology and folklore—particularly deities, the Fianna, and giants.

CHAPTER 7
Mythological Figures

The mythological figures of Irish Paganism were practically innumerable due to each tribe having their own deities and version of the Pagan religion. That said, there were some deities that were found in almost all the tribes and who were integral to the mythological cycles that were formalized in writing by Catholic monks from the 11th century A.C.E. onwards. In this chapter, we will explore these figures and other figures that may have become important in Irish mythology after Paganism became a minority belief system.

The Tuatha Dé Danann

The clan of Nemed were the predecessors of

the Tuatha Dé Danann. Their founder, Nemed, had come from a region beside the Black Sea with his wife and thousands of followers. They traveled to lush Ireland and established homes and villages there. He hired four Fomorians (giant pirates) to build a castle for him in each quarter of the island. Once they had built the castles, he killed them, thus exacting revenge on the rest of the Fomorians.

The Fomorians sent forces to wage battle with the Nemedians, with the conflict being violent and persistent. Some Nemedians were swept away by the sea during the warfare and carried to the lands that make up Denmark and its islands today. Other Nemedians could see their defeat coming and abandoned Ireland to travel and find a new home—which they established in the mountains of Greece. The Fomorians, as the victors, left a group of their own to control the land, while the bulk of their forces returned to their home beneath the waves to the north of Ireland.

The Nemedians who established their home in Greece, who had become known as the Fir Bolg, worked as manual laborers for generations. They grew tired of eking out an existence, deciding to steal the ships and head back to their ancestral home. Once there, they established themselves at the mouths of five Irish rivers and moved inland, taking back control of the island from the weak Fomorians who had been left to control the island.

After settling in the Danish lands, the other group learned about the occult from poet teachers in the four cities of Fálias, Foirias, Fionnias, and Muirias. The poet teachers were Mórfheasa (in Fálias), Easras (from Foirias), Uiscias (from Fionnias), and Séimhias (from Muirias). The four poets taught the Tuatha Dé Danann all they knew, until they were better at the arts of pagan cunning than their teachers). The arts were druidism, magic, devilry, knowledge, and prophecy. There were also tokens from each city that were provided to the Nemedian group. The tokens became the four treasures of the Tuatha Dé Danann (as they were known when they left back to Ireland) and were important to their identity as a nation once they re-established their presence in Ireland—now as a race with magical abilities and heightened strength. Tuatha Dé Danann is translated to the "people of the goddess Danu." They had become a supernatural, magic-wielding race through their training.

The four treasures were the Lia Fáil, on which the kings of Ireland would later be proclaimed. It would cry out whenever a new king took over the rule of Ireland. It is currently on the Hill of Tara where the ancient High Kings were inaugurated. The Claiomh Solais, translated to the "Sword of Light," was wielded by the first king of the Tuatha Dé Danann, Nuada. When he used it, no opponent he faced could escape its wrath. The Cauldron of the Dagda was the third of these tokens. It could never be depleted and would provide food for the massive feasts of the god of hospitality and abundance. The final token was the Spear of Lugh, Sleá Lúgh, that was wielded by the god of light, Lugh. It would always hit its target and was an indomitable force in battle.

When the Tuatha Dé Danann landed in what is now Leitrim in Ireland, there was a fog that lasted for days. They burned their ships so that they could not return to the lands of their learning, and when the smoke and fog lifted, they sent out a party of representatives who met with representatives of the Fir Bolg. The Tuatha Dé Danann wanted half the island, which the Fir Bold was not prepared to offer. Thus, the First Battle of the Mag Tuired commenced. Ultimately the Tuatha Dé Danann won and gave the Fir Bolg Connaught, taking the rest of Ireland for themselves.

Ultimately the Tuatha Dé Danann ruled Ireland successfully for many generations. They held power until the Milesians invaded and beat them after the Second Battle of Mag Tuired. At the point of victory, the Milesians offered the Tuatha Dé Danann a contract in which the latter would refrain from living in the human world of Ireland and would retreat their populations to the Otherworld. A list will follow of the most prominent Tuatha Dé Danann from before, during, and after the height of their control over the nation.

Danu

Danu was the mother goddess of the divine beings of the Tuatha Dé Danann race. She gave birth to the generation of deities that would later go on to expand the race. Thus, she was the mother of her nation. As such, she was the goddess of fertility, femininity, and motherhood. She suckled the babies of the gods to provide them with her power. She was skilled with magic and was particularly good at controlling water and wind.

Dagda

The Dagda was one of the most important gods of the Gaelic pantheon. He was the father of many of the other gods and of many warriors. His main realm was agriculture and fertility in relation to food and plenty. He was the custodian of the Cauldron of Plenty and would host large feasts where all could eat their fill. As such, he was also a god of hospitality and generosity, within limits. If someone abused the hospitality that was provided to them, he would punish them.

One of his neighbors took advantage of his hospitality at a time by eating the same amount of food that would come from three boars each day. To teach him a lesson, the Dagda put gold coins in his food and the man died when his stomach couldn't process it. While the Dagda was almost killed as a result for violating hospitality rules (since he was accused of poisoning a guest), he proved it was gold that had killed the man—and in the process he taught the valuable lesson of appreciating the hospitality you're provided with.

This tied in with his duty as a god of natural law and order. He was considered a fair god, but he would dole out death when he deemed it necessary. His capacity for delivering death was potent, with him making a potent fiend on the battlefield. He was a warrior of great wisdom and strength, and the added capacity of good control over magic. His magical capability was far above the others as he was the head of all druids.

He was described as being large, but with clothes that were too small, thus having an unkempt appearance. His hair and beard were messy, and he looked foolish. Despite this, he was described as being friendly, welcoming, and powerful.

Brigid

Brigid was a daughter of the Dagda and Danu. She was a goddess of fire and the sun, thus she had bright red hair. As a sun goddess, she had power over fertility, particularly in relation to agriculture. Spring was her realm of power, which put her in the favor of the later Irish population—hence her reputation as a kind-hearted and motherly deity. Her powers included capability with art, crafts, and poetry, which meant that she was a vital power in the pursuits of many of the working-class Irish.

Despite being kind-hearted, she could also be violent when it came to protecting what was important. She taught people to stand on their own two feet and was a capable warrior who led by example. Due to the dual nature of her power, she had a beautiful half to her face representing her roles in relation to spring and motherhood, while she also had an ugly half that showed the violent nature of her warrior spirit. Her ugly side warned of death in the same way the appearance of a banshee did.

Neit

Neit was one of the sons of the Dagda and Danu. He was a husband of two of the goddesses who made up the Morrigan. Just like the Morrigan, he was a war deity. In battle, his ferocity and passion were characteristic of his fighting style. The violence inherent in his nature was appropriate as he was originally a Fomorian. After fathering multiple other Fomorians, he changed his allegiance to the Tuatha Dé Danann.

Midir

He was a son of the Dagda and Danu who was responsible for forming many of the lakes and rivers of the countryside. He was a capable magician who displayed intelligence in the things he did and created. He was of noble appearance, with a circlet of gold in his blonde hair and gem-encrusted shield. The story of his pursuit of Étain has cemented him into the culture of the Irish, showing the lengths a man would go through if he genuinely loved a woman.

Ainé

Ainé was a goddess of wealth who was born to the Dagda and Dany. She was the goddess of summer, thus making her a goddess of the sun and fertility as well. She was a goddess of plenty in relation to harvests and crops, as well as a goddess of love. In a myth of the king of Munster, Ailill, raping her, she bit off his ear and made him ineligible to continue holding the kingship as a result. At this point, she became a goddess of sovereignty because was now able to influence the rulership of the nation.

Cermait

Cermait was a son of the Dagda and Danu who was best known for having an affair with Lugh's wife. When Lugh found out, he killed the god, leaving the three children of his affair fatherless. When the three children—mac Ceacht, mac Gréine, and mac Cuill—grew up, they slew Lugh. They took over his role as king of the Tuatha Dé Danann and became the last kings before the race agreed to migrate to the Otherworld. The three cycled the kingship, holding the position for one year each over a period of 29 years until the Second Battle of Mag Tuired.

Nechtan

Nechtan was a god who held custody of the Well of Wisdom. The well was situated under nine chestnut trees who imparted wisdom with their fruit. In the well was the Salmon of

Wisdom which ate all the chestnuts as they fell in the water. It was a sacred place from where Fionn mac Cumhail ate the salmon and became the wisest warrior in Irish history. When Nechtan's wife violated the sanctity of the well by walking around it clockwise, the well spat out the water that carved the River Boyne into the countryside. In the process she lost an eye and limbs, eventually dying in the river's flow to the ocean.

Nuada

Nuada (also called Elcmar) was the first king of the Tuatha Dé Danann and led his people when they arrived in their ships. In the First Battle of Mag Tuired, he lost his hand, which made him ineligible to hold the title of king. A hand of silver was made for him by Dian Cécht, but this only aided his capacity as a warrior, not his eligibility as a king. Dian Cécht's son then used magic to reattach his original hand, which made him whole and allowed him to claim back his title from the tyrant Fomorian king, Bres. His second reign was a period of generous and fair rule—a period in stark contrast with the rule of Bres. Nuada was also known as a god of hunting and fishing, contributing to his capacity of being generous.

Boann

Boann was the goddess of the River Boyne. She provided fertility with her waters, and she was an individual of great knowledge and poetic ability. When she was the wife of Nuada, she had an affair with the Dagda and didn't want her husband to find out. The Dagda grabbed the sun and made a single day that was nine months long so that she would have their child after a single day of pregnancy. As such, Nuada didn't notice the affair as he wasn't aware the pregnancy took place on that day.

The child, Aengus Óg, was put in the care of Midir, who raised him to prevent Aengus finding out about the infidelity and taking out his anger on the child. Boann later became the wife of Nechtan, the custodian of the Well of Wisdom. When she failed to respect her husband's warnings, she disrespected the well and lost her life in the process. In the process she created the River Boyne, which was imbued with her essence.

Aengus Óg

Aengus Óg was the son of the Dagda and Boann. He was the god of youthful love who, as such, had mastery of poetry and cunning use of words to woo his lovers. He was a god of youth who had powers over life and death. He could resurrect the dead and provide youth to those he deemed fit. Further, his power over youth gave him the good looks of a young man. However, being human wasn't his only form, as illustrated in the myth of the dream of Aengus.

In this myth, he dreamed of a beautiful woman who he fell in love with instantly. He couldn't find this girl anywhere, so he employed the help of other deities. He found her after two years with the help of a king who located her whereabouts. She was in a group of 150 women who were chained to turn into swans on a lakeshore for a festival. They would remain swans for a whole year. Aengus made a deal with the captors that he could keep her if he identified her in swan form. When all the women turned into swans, he transfigured himself too, calling out to find her. When they located each other, they flew off while singing a song that was so beautiful that it put the captors to sleep for three days.

Morrigan

Morrigan was the goddess of death and destiny. She was a warrior goddess made up of three sisters (Badb, Macha, and Nemain) in one form. Her powers extended to being a provider of prophecies that would show people their fate. In battle she would circle the warriors as a crow and eat the remains of the dead. As a human, she was beautiful and could seduce men easily. She could hold many forms, being a shapeshifter, with the four main forms being that of a maiden, a fierce warrior queen, a crone, and a raven. On occasion she would appear as an old washerwoman that scrubbed the bloody clothes clean of those who had fallen in battle.

Her first personage, Badb, was a war goddess who had the human appearance of a crone. She would make men on the battlefield confused and frightened if they opposed those she favored. She was known as a death bringer, killing men with terror when she cried out as a crow.

The second personage was Macha, who was also a war goddess. Her powers extended to being an earth goddess, and a goddess of horses and cows. Maternal reproductivity, agrarian fruitfulness, and sexual fertility were all associated with her. Her most famous myth revolves around her giving the men of Ulster a curse of falling asleep and feeling menstrual cramps because they didn't intervene when a king put her and her unborn children in danger. The danger was caused by forcing her to run a race against the king's prized horse while she was pregnant and not allowing her to stop when she went into labor with twins.

The third personage of Morrigan was Nemain, the goddess of madness in battle. She would fly above battlefields and terrorize warriors. Her monstrous shriek was akin to that of a banshee and signaled the death of many people. She used her power over fear to debilitate the enemies of warriors and forces she favored.

Manaanán mac Lir

Also known as Lir, he was a sea god who ruled the island paradises of the Otherworld. He protected sailors and provided abundant crops to those under his custodianship. He used his swine to give immortality to those who ate them, even bringing gods back to life with them. He had a magnificent chariot that he could ride across the water and a suit of armor that was impenetrable.

When Badb was chosen as the king of the Tuatha Dé Danann after their defeat by the Milesians, he was displeased. As such, he didn't join with the rest of them, but created his own sidhe away on his islands. Áeb, a moon goddess associated with the growth of flowers and plants, was offered to him as a wife by Badb as a gesture of goodwill. They were happy and had four children, but she died giving birth to a pair of their twins. Badb offered him another wife, Aoife, who became the stepmother of the children.

She wasn't happy with the attention the children were given by their father, so she carried out a plan that turned the four children into swans. Lir followed his children and formed a settlement around the lake where they lived. Badb joined him at the lake, where they all lived for 300 years. The swan-children flew away and lived on a sea for 300 years, and a different lake for a further 300 years. When they flew back over their father's settlement after 600 years away, they saw he wasn't there any longer—the Tuatha Dé Danann had settled in other parts of the Otherworld.

Lugh

Lugh was the second king of the Tuatha Dé Danann, despite being half-Fomorian himself. He held the all-powerful abilities of controlling storms and the sun and was powerful beyond comprehension. He helped incite the revolt against the Fomorian king of the Tuatha Dé Danann, Bres, when he ruled with tyranny after king Nuada lost his hand. Lugh managed to kill Balor of the Evil Eye to avenge his killing of king Nuada.

Lugh was a god of nobility who was expert in

the matters of rulership. He held people to their contracts and gave swift judgment to anyone that broke their oaths or the law. Further, he was an impressive warrior of vitality who wielded the Spear of Assal. None could stand against him if he was their foe in a conflict as he was willing to lie and cheat to win in fights he deemed important. His expertise extended from fighting to matters of language and craft, making him a skilled artisan and poet.

Sovereignty

Sovereignty was the spirit of the Earth. She could decide who should be the ruler of Ireland. When a king met her expectations, the land would be fertile, and the nation would win at war. But should he fall short, she would punish the land with failed crops and losses. New kings were symbolically married to her when they were crowned. During the ceremony, he would be expected to promise that he would protect and maintain the land and his people. Fertility and abundance were her gifts for his loyalty to this oath. Holy wells and horses were both associated with her.

Étain

She was originally a princess of Ulster in her first life. She was in love with the god Midir, who was already married. His wife took offense to their affair and transfigured her into multiple forms, eventually settling on a fly. The fly was blown away and swallowed by a distant queen. After swallowing the fly, the queen grew pregnant and gave birth nine months later. Reborn, Étain had no recollection of her first life, so she was married off to the High King. She was found by Midir in her new life, who pursued her once more. She fell in love with him again but remained faithful to the king.

Midir challenged the High King to a game of fidchell, with a kiss from Étain being the prize should he win. The High King agreed, but he lost and the time came for the kiss, he reneged and brought in military forces to seize Midir. The god changed both him and Étain into swans and they went into hiding while the High King went on a rampage in which he destroyed many sidhe while looking for his wife. He found them eventually, and Midir said he would give her back if the king chose her correctly from 50 versions that had been created of his queen. The king chose incorrectly, at which point he agreed to leave Midir and Étain alone to live a life together.

Through this process she became a goddess of transformation, rebirth, and love. Dawn, rain, and the sun are some of the important associations with her, especially in relation to their ability to produce or highlight transformation. Her role extended to responsibility for healing people when they were ill and transporting their souls to the afterlife when they died.

The (Potentially) Sacrificial Trio: Taranis, Teutates, and Esus

The sacred triad consisted of three Gaelic gods: Taranis, Teutates, and Esus. They are currently believed to have been the three gods to whom human sacrifice was approved of, with each requiring a different form of sacrifice.

Taranis was the god of thunder, storms, and bad weather. This meant that powers could directly impact the lives of farmers, making it important to keep him appeased. His symbols were his thunderbolt and a wheel. Tuetates was a god of the people. In other words, he was the god believed to hold the tribe together as a community. Esus was the god of mastery and lordship, particularly in relation to a skill or zone of influence in your life. He was associated with egrets, cranes, and sacred bulls.

Dian Cécht

He was the gods' physician. He was able to cure anyone by throwing them in a well and pulling them back out. He helped make the silver hand of Nuada but was jealous of his son's ingenuity when he managed to reattach Nuada's original hand using magic. The jealousy drove Dian Cécht to murder his own son.

Bodach

The bodach is the storm hag's husband, and he holds just as much power. He might look like an old, poor farmer, but he is in fact the king of Mag Mell (the realm of paradise where you don't age). Together, he and the storm hag parented the banshees of the world. The capabilities of the banshees likely come from his capacity to foresee when disaster and death will take place. Despite his large responsibility as the king of Mag Mell and his power as the consort of the storm hag, he still enjoys moments of trivial mischief.

Climbing down chimneys to poke you awake while you sleep is a favorite pastime of the bodach. If he can't get in through the chimney, he'll come in through open windows or a crack in the walls. You might not realize why you're having such a distressing night of no sleep because he appears in the form of a shadow that can flit back and forth throughout the house. In his eyes, we are silly creatures and the trivial games he plays aren't of much consequence because he's privy to far more important matters, namely the deaths that people will face one day.

The Fianna

The Fianna were a fierce group of warriors who provided for themselves by hunting and trading things from the wild. They had a high moral standard and demanded competence from their members. The position you held was a lifelong commitment, with intense criteria to meet if you wanted to join. Most of the stories in the Fenian Cycle were made up of their exploits.

Near the end of their existence, they started losing sight of their values of honor and started getting too high an opinion of themselves. This is represented in the story of how they were wiped out. The band of warriors were supposed to get a tribute when the granddaughter of the high king married her fiancé. He was killed before the wedding took place, making the tribute unnecessary. The Fianna refused to leave without their tribute and created a commotion with the princess and her family.

The High King's son then raised an army and waged war with the warriors. They fought as well as they could, but the sheer numbers they faced overpowered them, thus wiping out the greatest fighters Ireland had ever seen.

Fionn mac Cumhail

Fionn mac Cumhail, also known as Fionn MacCool, was a warrior and hunter who held the final position of leadership of the Fianna. He was strong and clever, with his wisdom being enhanced when he ate the Salmon of knowledge. In addition to being a warrior, he could also transform into a giant. The story of how he created the Giant's Causeway is the most famous detailing his dual life as a giant.

As the story goes, he created the causeway so that he could reach another giant named Benandonner in Scotland to fight with him. When he got there, he saw the other giant fast asleep, and he realized how much bigger the Scottish giant was. He thus ran back to Ireland, where his wife came up with a plan to keep the other giant from causing problems.

His wife, Oona, was also a giant, so she wrapped up her husband in a blanket and made it as if Fionn was her baby. When Benandonner arrived in Ireland, he saw the "baby" and immediately grew frightened of how large the father must be. Thus, he ran back to Scotland, tearing up the middle part of the causeway as he went.

Giants

There were many giants in Irish mythology.

Most of them were humans with the ability to transform into giants, while a few were permanently giants. Some of the most famous ones are noted below.

Amergin mac Eccit

He was a giant who had grown mad at the men of Erin. As such, he decided to attack them by throwing boulders and lumps of earth at them. His supernatural strength made it possible for him to pick up rocks that far outweighed any of the men he was facing. His career was as a warrior poet, and he is known as the individual who slayed the three-headed monster Ellén Trechen.

Iliach

Iliach was Amergin mac Eccit's brother. He also attacked the men of Errin. First, he threw weapons until all the weapons he could lay hands upon were exhausted. He then threw boulders and clumps of earth at them. When he couldn't lay his hands on anything else, he even pulverized the bodies of those he had killed and threw balls of human flesh at his enemy.

Dryantore

Dryantore was both a giant and a magician. He is known to have been one of the few individuals who managed to capture the Fianna.

In the myth of their capture, his two sons and brother-in-law had been killed by Fionn mac Cumhail in battle. His sister, Ailna, was also a giant and she had come to her brother so they could exact revenge for the deaths. To do this, he caught Fionn mac Cumhail and some of his companions using magical music that made them powerless. Once powerless and asleep, he imprisoned them in a cell.

Fionn and his companions escaped using trickery, and when Alina saw they escaped, she died of chagrin. With her out of the picture, the warriors killed Dryantore and feasted in his castle. After their meals and a good night's rest, they were returned to the realms of men.

Cú Chulainn

He was the best warrior of the Red Branch, the elite military wing of the king of Ulster. They were loyal to the king, but not necessarily to the High King of all Ireland. Cú Chulainn was a son of Lugh, the god of light and the sun and Dechtire, the daughter of a druid. His mom got pregnant with Laugh after leaving her wedding with another man in the shape of a bird. She had Cú Chulainn and raised him for three years before returning to her home.

He grew up to be very large and with great strength. He had seven pupils per eye, seven fingers per hand, and seven toes per foot. The other men of Ulster were occasionally struck with a curse where they would fall asleep and experience menstrual pains for nine days at a time because of their lack of intervention when the goddess Macha had been forced to race against the king's horse while she was in the advanced stages of pregnancy. The Gaelic deities like Cú Chulainn and the competence he showed as a warrior so much that they exempted him from this curse.

He performed feats of strength and good character. In battles, he would go into fits of rage and berserk hordes of enemies. He single-handedly defended Ulster against the forces of the queen of Connaught at age 17. We can confidently say that he is one of the best-known warriors of Irish mythology.

Cú Roí mac Dáire

Cú Roí was a human king who had supernatural powers. One of them was to increase in height and to become beefier, making him a giant. One day he transformed into a commoner, and then into a giant form of this commoner. Three nights were prompted to cut his head off in this form and eagerly went for the opportunity because he disgusted them in this form. Cú Chulainn defended the vagabond-looking giant, teaching the moral that there's more to things than your status and looks; there's also goodness.

Fomorians

This was a race of supernatural giants. They were one of the earliest races to settle Ireland. Known to be monstrous, deformed, and ugly, they yet held power over the forces of nature—especially destructive ones like plagues. They came from a land under the sea to the north of Ireland.

Normally bloodthirsty and fond of war, they enslaved those they conquered where they went. Their biggest foes were the Tuatha Dé Danann, who waged war against them. Bres, one of the Femorians, became the king of the Tuatha Dé Danann when their king lost his hand. When the tyranny of Bres was put to a stop by ousting him, the Fomorians took offense, leading to the Second Battle of Mag Tuired.

Some of the most famous ones are listed below.

Bres

Bres was an exception to the norm of ugliness. Be was beautiful beyond compare, but the beauty was skin deep. He took over the role of the king of the Tuatha Dé Danann in an attempt to repair the relationship between the two races. But his suppression using unfair taxation created famine and strife for those under his rule because they couldn't keep enough resources together to live comfortably. This led to the Tuatha Dé Danann ousting him when Angus Oh gave them the courage needed to revolt.

Domnu

She was one of the evilest Fomorians. Her supernatural role was to oppose light and goodness. In carrying out this role, she gave birth to many of the Fomorians who would later fight against the Tuatha Dé Danann.

Balor

Perhaps one of the best-known Fomorians, Balor had an eye that was altered by a potion that generated evil while he was a child. The eye gained the ability to kill or poison anything it looked at, thus making it the embodiment of evil. He was a supernatural figure who represented darkness and wickedness.

Ethniu

She was a daughter of Balor. It was foretold that she would give birth to a child that would overthrow him, so he imprisoned her in a tower so that she wouldn't get pregnant. Balor made the mistake of stealing the cow of the deity Cian, so Cian broke Ethniu out of the tower. He then impregnated her, so she gave birth to triplets, but Balor killed two of them by drowning to keep his kingship safe. The third, Lugh, survived and eventually fulfilled the prophecy that had led his grandfather to kill his siblings.

The figures in this chapter lead storied lives that gave us lessons we can live by. Whether they were cruel or kind, their message impacted on those who listened, leading to inspiration and warning. In the next chapter, we will explore how the collection of Irish history, beliefs, and mythology have impacted the Ireland of today.

CONCLUSION

In this book, we first looked at the lives of the prehistoric people of Ireland. They may have been simple, but the ingenuity they had in facing the problems of their lives with the tools at their disposal was astounding. First, they developed tools of stone, then copper, bronze, and finally iron. Throughout this, they developed international trade routes and intricate belief systems based on oral tradition. A characteristic body of art was developed during this period that's still characteristic of Ireland today. During the Iron Age, the Gaels settled alongside the prehistoric people of Ireland, forming a complex society that still intrigues us today.

They were the first race of Irish settlers to

leave a written mark—a mark that provided insight into their beliefs and what they held important. They also advanced the art, architecture, religion, and government of the ancient nations of the island. The ideas and beliefs they developed were mainly written down by later Christian settlers who created centers of learning in their monasteries. As such, there were some alterations to those teachings. But, when read with a pinch of salt, those alterations can be bypassed, leading to an interpretation of the underlying Gaelic convictions. Yet, myths weren't restricted to those earlier Gaelic times. There are famous myths that stem from the early Christian period as well.

One such was that the goddess Brigid was believed to have converted to Christianity, thus becoming the patron saint that's now celebrated throughout Ireland. Another was that St. Patrick was said to have vanquished multiple giant wyrms, along with the other snakes that lived on the island. These myths were later incorporated into the Lebor Gabála alongside earlier Gaelic myths. The earlier Gaelic myths were incorporated into the Four Mythological Cycles that you can use today to systematically study Irish mythology.

The first of the four cycles revolves around the Tuatha Dé Danann and their exploits. Many of the most impressive figures of Irish mythology are included here, such as Nuada (the first king of the gods). The second was the Ulster cycle, which detailed heroic tales of the first century in Ulster and Leinster. The Fenian cycle was the third, which described the exploits of Fionn mac Cumhaill and his legendary band of warriors, the Fianna. Impressive myths recounting battles with giants and all types of creatures that the Fianna had to face and overcome were chronicled in this cycle. The final cycle described the lives of the High Kings of Ireland and their families as told by court poets for generations.

The Gaelic people further left Ireland with its most important Pagan festivals. These were the Imbolc, Beltane, Lughnasa, and Samhain, which concerned important times during the agricultural year. More specifically, they marked changes of the seasons and the significance those seasons had or would have on the harvests of farmers. The Ostara, Litha, Mabon, and Yule festivals are also ancient festivals, but with more significance in relation to the cycle of the sun through the year. These festivals take place on the two solstices and equinoxes of the year.

The early Christian period was followed by continuous invasions and attempts at subjugation by the Vikings, then the Normans, and finally the English Crown. The period when the English Crown was directly in control of Ireland (since the rule of King Henry VIII was perhaps the most difficult period of Irish history, especially for Catholics and individuals of Gaelic descent. Under Queen Mary and Queen Elizabeth I the plantations in which Scottish, English, and Welsh people were moved to displace many of the local Irish. The displacements and the usage of the land in the Pale by the English-controlled government and their loyal subjects relegated the Irish to lower quality lands.

Things became more difficult for the native population due to the lack of care by their British overlords, leading to untold harm in the following centuries. The Potato Famine was the breaking point of negligence, leading to the deaths of more than a million people. An exodus of people from Ireland followed as a result, with most emigrants leaving for the United States. While the suppression and negligence of the Irish nation led to many deaths and people abandoning their homeland, it also led to the spread of Irish ideas and beliefs to the rest of the world.

Those ideas included the mythology and the Pagan beliefs that had been with the Irish nation from before the times of the Celts. It's a body of stories that imparted lessons that still positively impact and unify the Irish today.

Use the knowledge you now have of Irish history and mythology to raise respect for the identity of this nation. It's a worldwide nation sharing its history, beliefs, and lessons across the globe.

REFERENCES

About: Fiacha mac Delbaíth. (n.d.). DBPedia. Retrieved February 11, 2023, from https://dbpedia.org/page/Fiacha_mac_Delba%C3%ADth

About: Mag Mell. (n.d.). DBPedia. Retrieved February 13, 2023, from https://dbpedia.org/page/Mag_Mell

Áine the goddess who took revenge on a king. (n.d.). Ireland Information. https://www.ireland-information.com/irish-mythology/aine-irish-legend.html

All about Eostre - The Pagan goddess of dawn. (2020, March 5). Arcane Alchemy. http://www.arcane-alchemy.com/blog/2020/3/5/all-about-eostre-the-pagan-goddess-of-dawn#:~:text=Eostre%20is%20the%20Germanic%20goddess

All about Eostre || The Pagan goddess of dawn. (2020). [Video]. YouTube. https://www.youtube.com/watch?v=h57XfAeX9F0&t=449s

Allen, R. (2019a, May 22). Dechtire. God checkers. https://www.godchecker.com/irish-mythology/DECHTIRE/#:~:text=She%20is%20the%20daughter%20of,So%20she%20did.

Allen, R. (2019b, May 23). Fúamnach (P. J. Allen & C. Saunders, Eds.). God Checker. https://www.godchecker.com/irish-mythology/FUAMNACH/

Allen, R. (2019c, May 23). Fúamnach (P. J. Allen & C. Saunders, Eds.). God Checker. https://www.godchecker.com/irish-mythology/FUAMNACH/

Alp-Luachra. (n.d.). Emerald Isle. https://emeraldisle.ie/alp-luachra-

Ancient Irish Games. (n.d.). Twinkl. https://www.twinkl.co.za/teaching-wiki/ancient-irish-games

Angevin Empire. (2023). Encyclopedia Britannica. https://www.britannica.com/place/Angevin-empire

Aos Si. (n.d.). Mythical Creatures Guide. https://www.mythicalcreaturesguide.com/aos-si/

Aos Sí. (2021, August 24). Wikipedia. Retrieved February 2, 2023 from https://en.wikipedia.org/wiki/Aos_S%C3%AD

Art of dry stone walling, knowledge and techniques. (n.d.). UNESCO. https://ich.unesco.org/en/RL/art-of-dry-stone-walling-knowledge-and-techniques-01393

Atma Flare. (2019, August 22). Indech, treacherous fomorian general. Tumblr. https://atmaflare.tumblr.com/post/187181853478/indech-treacherous-fomorian-general-in-irish

Augustyn, A. (2023). Bronze Age. Britannica. https://www.britannica.com/event/Bronze-Age

Barone, F. (2020, March 12). Luck of the Irish: Folklore and fairies in rural Ireland. Human Relations Area Files. https://hraf.yale.edu/luck-of-the-irish-folklore-and-fairies-in-rural-ireland/#:~:text=Known%20to%20the%20islanders%20as

Bhagat, D. (2018, October 30). The origins and practices of: Samhain,

Día de los Muertos, and All Saints Day. Boston Public Library. https://www.bpl.org/blogs/post/the-origins-and-practices-of-holidays-samhain-dia-de-los-muertos-and-all-saints-day/#:~:text=Samhain%20is%20observed%20from%20sunset

Bhagat, D. (2019, June 18). The origins and practices of Litha. Boston Public Library. https://www.bpl.org/blogs/post/the-origins-and-practices-of-litha/

Blackie, S. (2016, November 15). The dangerous women of Irish Mythology. Dangerous Women Project. https://dangerouswomenproject.org/2016/11/15/the-dangerous-women-of-irish-mythology/

Blakely, S. (2021, May 14). Copper age history & society | Chalcolithic age features. Study. https://study.com/academy/lesson/copper-age-history.html

Boan, Goddess of the Boyne. (n.d.). Discover Boyne Valley. https://www.discoverboynevalley.ie/boyne-valley-drive/heritage-sites/boann-goddess-boyne

Brehon Academy. (2022). Irish mythology deep dive: The mythological cycle 6+ hours. [Video]. YouTube. https://www.youtube.com/watch?v=fZhYc8l6v00&t=488s

Brú na Bóinne - Archaeological ensemble of the Bend of the Boyne. (n.d.). UNESCO World Heritage Convention. https://whc.unesco.org/en/list/659/#:~:text=The%20three%20main%20prehistoric%20sites

Buckles, N. (n.d.). The legend of Ellén Trechend. Nifty Buckles. https://niftybuckles.buzz/2018/07/26/aillen-trechenn/

Bunbury, T. (2020, March 21). What did the Romans ever do for Ireland? The Irish Times. https://www.irishtimes.com/culture/books/what-did-the-romans-ever-do-for-ireland-1.4205876#:~:text=The%20Romans%20never%20conquered%20Ireland,%E2%80%9Ctrackless%20wastes%E2%80%9Dof%20Galloway

Butler, I. (2020, January 13). Ireland's ancient burial mounds. Europe up Close. https://europeupclose.com/article/irelands-ancient-burial-mounds/

BYU Department of Anthropology. (2014). Barry Cunliffe: Who were the Celts? [Video]. YouTube. https://www.youtube.com/watch?v=G8FM9nMFbfI&t=17s

Caitlin. (2021, September 7). Cat sìth: including 5 legendary tales. Highland Titles. https://www.highlandtitles.com/blog/cat-sith/

Caitlin. (2022, February 11). Everything you need to know about Tír na nÓg. Celtic Titles. https://www.celtictitles.com/blog/tir-na-nog/

Campbell, J. F. (1890). Fachan. Popular tales of the west Highlands (Vol. IV, pp. 297–298). Encyclopedia Mythica. https://pantheon.org/articles/f/fachan.html

Cannon, J. (2015). Overview: Kingdom of the Isles. A Dictionary of British History. Oxford University Press. https://www.oxfordreference.com/display/10.1093/oi/authority.20110803100012518

Carmody, I. Ób. (2016, April 16). The story of Rúadán from Cath Maige

Tuired. Story Archeology. https://storyarchaeology.com/the-story-of-ruadan-from-cath-maige-tuired-2/
Casey, L. (2022, December 4). The Irish legend of the pooka. Irish Central. https://www.irishcentral.com/roots/history/irish-legend-pooka#:~:text=The%20Pooka%2C%20or%20in%20Irish,%2C%20Channel%20Islands%2C%20and%20Brittany
Castlehunter. (2012, May 27). The fairy castle co Dublin. Ireland in Ruins. http://irelandinruins.blogspot.com/2012/05/fairy-castle-co-dublin.html
Cataliotti, J. (2022, November 11). Copper age tools. Study.com. https://study.com/academy/lesson/copper-age-weapons-tools.html#:~:text=The%20metal%20was%20far%20more
Celtic art. (n.d.). The Artist. https://www.theartist.me/art-movement/celtic-art/
Celtic Otherworld. (2022, March 25). Celtic Life. https://celticlifeintl.com/celtic-otherworld/
Cermait. (n.d.). Myths and Folklore Wiki. Retrieved February 11, 2023, from https://mythus.fandom.com/wiki/Cermait
Cermait. (2022, April 14). Wikipedia. Retrieved February 11, 2023 from https://en.wikipedia.org/wiki/Cermait
Christianity arrives in Ireland. (2020, March 2). Your Irish Culture. https://www.yourirish.com/history/christianity/arrival-of-christianity
Cist. (n.d.). Merriam-Webster. https://www.merriam-webster.com/dictionary/cist
Cliodhna. (n.d.). Bard Mythologies. https://bardmythologies.com/cliodhna/
Clíodhna of the banshees. (n.d.). Ireland Information. https://www.ireland-information.com/irish-mythology/cliodhna-irish-legend.html
Copper. (n.d.). National Museum of Ireland. https://microsites.museum.ie/bronzeagehandlingbox/object-copper.html
Corbel. (n.d.). Merriam-Webster. https://www.merriam-webster.com/dictionary/corbel
Court tomb. (n.d.). Dictonary.com. https://www.dictionary.com/browse/court-tomb
Creidhne. (n.d.). The White Goddess. http://www.thewhitegoddess.co.uk/divinity_of_the_day/irish/creidhne.asp
Crom Cruach, the dark god of the burial mound. (2016, October 1). An Sionnach Fionn. https://ansionnachfionn.com/2016/10/01/crom-cruach-the-dark-god-of-the-burial-mound/
Cú Chulainn. (2022). A. Tikkanen (Ed.), Encyclopedia Britannica. https://www.britannica.com/topic/Cu-Chulainn
Cummings, V. (2015). Dolmen. Britannica. https://www.britannica.com/topic/dolmen
Cymres, W. (n.d.). Brigid: Survival of a goddess. Druidry. https://druidry.org/resources/brigid-survival-of-a-goddess
D'Costa, K. (2013, March 31). Beyond Ishtar: The tradition of eggs at

Easter. Scientific American. https://blogs.scientificamerican.com/anthropology-in-practice/beyond-ishtar-the-tradition-of-eggs-at-easter/

Delbáeth. (n.d.). People Pill. https://peoplepill.com/people/delbaeth

Devine, B. (2013, August 27). Not all Celts are Gaels. The Wild Geese. https://thewildgeese.irish/profiles/blogs/not-all-celts-are-gaels#:~:text=%22Celt%22%20is%20the%20broader%20term

DHWTY. (2017, December 28). The Fomorians: Destructive giants of Irish legend. Ancient Origins. https://www.ancient-origins.net/myths-legends-europe/fomorians-destructive-giants-irish-legend-009349

Dian Cécht. (2018, February 15). Encyclopedia Britannica. https://www.britannica.com/topic/Dian-Cecht

Dowd, M. (2015). The Archaeology of Caves in Ireland. Oxbow Books.

Duna. (2017). Encyclopedia Britannica. https://www.britannica.com/topic/Danu

E, I. (2022a, September 20). They might be giants: 10 colossal Celts of Irish myth & legend. Irish Myths. https://irishmyths.com/2022/09/20/giants/

E, I. (2022b, September 26). Who is Balor of the Evil Eye? A brief biography of Irish mythology's "big Bbd." Irish Myths. https://irishmyths.com/2022/09/26/balor/

Early Christian Ireland. (n.d.). Ask about Ireland. Retrieved January 20, 2023 from https://www.askaboutireland.ie/learning-zone/primary-students/subjects/history/history-the-full-story/early-christian-ireland/#:~:text=Early%20Christian%20Ireland%20is%20the

Early Christian Ireland facts. (2022, January 11). Twinkl. https://www.twinkl.co.za/blog/early-christian-ireland-facts

Easter Rising. (n.d.). History. https://www.history.com/topics/british-history/easter-rising

Ehistoryadmin. (2014, May 9). "Ireland's greatest family": The Fitzgeralds, earls of Kildare. Kildare. https://kildare.ie/ehistory/index.php/irelands-greatest-family-the-fitzgeralds-earls-of-kildare/#:~:text=The%20earldom%20was%20created%20on

Elatha, Bres, Indech & Tethra: Rulers of the Fomorians. (n.d.). Atlas Mythica. https://atlasmythica.com/elatha-bres-indech-tethra-rulers-fomorians/

Ellén Trechend. (2009). Monstropedia. https://www.monstropedia.org/index.php?title=Ell%C3%A9n_Trechend

Ernmas. (2022, June 8). Wikipedia. Retrieved February 11, 2023 from https://en.wikipedia.org/wiki/Ernmas

Esus. (2015). Encyclopedia Britannica. https://www.britannica.com/topic/Esus

Etain. (n.d.). Bard Mythologies. https://bardmythologies.com/etain/

Far darrig facts for kids. (2022). Kiddle Encyclopedia. https://kids.kiddle.co/Far_darrig

Fergus. (2017, February 20). Enigmatic structures: Ireland's megalithic wedge tombs. The Irish Place.

https://www.theirishplace.com/heritage/enigmatic-structures-irelands-megalithic-wedge-tombs/

FilmRise Documentaries. (2014a). The Celts - BBC series, episode 1 - In the beginning - Full episode. [Video]. YouTube. https://www.youtube.com/watch?v=AU1dKfMIEUQ&t=7s

FilmRise Documentaries. (2014b). The Celts - BBC series, Episode 2 - Heroes in defeat - Full episode. [Video]. YouTube. https://www.youtube.com/watch?v=OVovskAh5QA

FilmRise Documentaries. (2014c). The Celts - BBC series, episode 3 - Sacred groves - Full episode [Video]. YouTube. https://www.youtube.com/watch?v=GsHghGwdWNg

FilmRise Documentaries. (2014d). The Celts - BBC series, episode 4 - From Camelot to Christ - Full episode [Video]. YouTube. https://www.youtube.com/watch?v=lfY4-2zKY-g

FilmRise Documentaries. (2014e). The Celts - BBC series, episode 5 - Legend and reality - Full episode [Video]. YouTube. https://www.youtube.com/watch?v=W_l5yFlEYds

FilmRise Documentaries. (2014f). The Celts - BBC series, episode 6 - A dead song? - Full episode. [Video]. YouTube. https://www.youtube.com/watch?v=wl7X4A_mNeU

Fionn mac Cumhail. (n.d.). Discovering Ireland. https://www.discoveringireland.com/fionn-mac-cumhail/

Fire of Learning. (2018a). History of Ireland - Documentary. [Video]. YouTube. https://www.youtube.com/watch?v=fbJKanTrf8c

Fire of Learning. (2018b). History of Ireland (Part 2) documentary. [Video]. YouTube. https://www.youtube.com/watch?v=vFoxstHK-Kg&t=9s

Forsyth, S. (n.d.). Irish fairies. Celtic Wedding Rings. https://www.celtic-weddingrings.com/fairy-stories/irish-fairies

Fortress of Lugh. (n.d.). The Dagda - (Celtic mythology explained). [Video]. YouTube. https://www.youtube.com/watch?v=62DBOC5CQGo&t=10s

From hunger to harvest - The history of the ancient Celtic festival Lughnasa. (2022, July 29). IrishCentral. https://www.irishcentral.com/culture/history-celtic-festival-lughnasa

Gaelic Ireland: The unfolded exciting history throughout the centuries. (2022, August 4). Connolly Cove. https://www.connollycove.com/gaelic-ireland/

Goibhniu. (1998). Encyclopedia Britannica. https://www.britannica.com/topic/Goibhniu

Good Friday Agreement: What is it? (2022, December 16). BBC News. https://www.bbc.com/news/uk-northern-ireland-61968177

Graham, H. (n.d.). Celtic Reconstructionism. Druidry. https://druidry.org/resources/celtic-reconstructionism

Greenberg, M. (2020, November 3). Who was Midir in Irish mythology? Mythology Source. https://mythologysource.com/midir-irish-mythology/

Greenberg, M. (2021, January 18). Who was the Dagda in Irish mythology. Mythology Source. https://mythologysource.com/dagda-celtic-god/

Hare, J. B. (1911). The fairy-faith in Celtic countries by W. Y. Evans-Wentz [1911] [Review of the fairy-faith in Celtic countries, by W. Y. Evans-Wentz]. https://www.sacred-texts.com/neu/celt/ffcc/index.htm

Harris, K. (2019, April 1). Legendary grannies: Hags in Celtic myths. Curious Historian. https://curioushistorian.com/legendary-grannies-hags-in-celtic-myths#:~:text=According%20to%20Celtic%20folklore%2C%20hags

Haynie, D. (2016, March 17). 10 countries with the most Irish emigrants. US News. https://www.usnews.com/news/best-countries/articles/2016-03-17/10-countries-with-the-most-irish-emigrants

Hirst, K. K. (2019, April 29). Mount Sandel - Mesolithic Settlement in Ireland. Thought Co. https://www.thoughtco.com/mount-sandel-mesolithic-settlement-in-ireland-171665

How the Irish predict the weather. (n.d.). Ireland's Own. https://www.irelandsown.ie/how-the-irish-predict-the-weather/

Howells, C. (2022, October 18). The questing beast: The legendary Arthurian creature. Myth Bank. https://mythbank.com/the-questing-beast/

Iaconangelo, D. (2016, June 15). Why ancient butter keeps turning up in Irish bogs. The Christian Science Monitor. https://www.csmonitor.com/Science/Science-Notebook/2016/0615/Why-ancient-butter-keeps-turning-up-in-Irish-bogs

Ian. (2008, September 19). Fachan. Mysterious Britain and Ireland. https://www.mysteriousbritain.co.uk/folklore/fachan/

Illes, J. (2009). Nemain. Encyclopedia of Spirits: The Ultimate Guide to the Magic of Fairies, Genies, Demons, Ghosts, Gods & Goddesses. https://occult-world.com/nemain/

Incredible history of the Tuatha de Danann: Ireland's Most Ancient Race. (2023, January 15). Connolly Cove. https://www.connollycove.com/tuatha-de-danann/

Innes, A. D. (1912). A history of the British nation. TC & EC Jack. https://www.britainexpress.com/History/Henry-VII-and-Ireland.htm

Insular hand. (n.d.). Merriam-Webster. https://www.merriam-webster.com/dictionary/Insular%20hand

Ipbestiary. (2020, August 30). Ethniu. Tumblr. https://www.tumblr.com/lpbestiary/627909588308639744/ethniu-is-a-fomorian-from-irish-mythology-the

Ireland in the 19th century. (n.d.). Ask about Ireland. https://www.askaboutireland.ie/learning-zone/primary-students/subjects/history/history-the-full-story/ireland-in-the-19th-centu/#:~:text=Ireland%20in%20the%20early%201800s

Ireland: 4 reasons why its culture is important. (n.d.). Pruvo. https://www.pruvo.com/blog/ireland-4-reasons-why-its-culture-is-important/

Ireland's bog bodies. (2015, July 2). Claddagh Design. https://www.claddaghdesign.com/blogs/irish-interest/ireland-

bog-bodies#:~:text=A%20total%20of%2017%20bog,of%20ritual%20sacrifice%20described%20above.
Irish folklore: Mythical monsters and terrifying creatures. (2022, November 11). Connolly Cove. https://www.connollycove.com/mythical-monsters-in-irish-folklore/
Irish Free State declared. (2020, October 4). History. https://www.history.com/this-day-in-history/irish-free-state-declared
Irish mythological creatures. (n.d.). Twinkl. https://www.twinkl.co.za/teaching-wiki/irish-mythological-creatures
Irish myths and legends 101. (n.d.). Ireland 101. https://www.ireland101.com/page/irish-legends#:~:text=The%20Pooka%20(also%20known%20as
Irish weather lore and traditions. (n.d.). Twinkl. https://www.eskeretns.ie/uploads/1/2/7/1/127165924/roi-gy-29-irish-weather-lore-and-traditions_ver_1.pdf
Ireland. (n.d.). The magical east of Ireland – ancient places, scenic lakes and Rocky Mountains. Komoot. https://www.komoot.com/collection/1255857/the-magical-east-of-ireland-ancient-places-scenic-lakes-and-rocky-mountains
Iron. (n.d.). Royal Society of Chemistry. https://www.rsc.org/periodic-table/element/26/iron#:~:text=Iron%20is%20the%20fourth%20most
Iron Age people: Celts. (n.d.). Ask about Ireland. https://www.askaboutireland.ie/learning-zone/primary-students/subjects/history/history-the-full-story/irelands-early-inhabitant/iron-age-people-celts/
Join Tia McCaughey and Darragh Finlay for our Mabon/Autumn equinox celebration and retreat on Sunday the 8th of September, Anaverna House and Estate Ravensdale Co. Louth. (n.d.). Darragh Finlay. https://darraghfinlay.ie/mabon-autumn-equinox-celebration-and-retreat/
Jones, M. (2004). Bean Sídhe. Jones' Celtic Encyclopedia. https://www.ancienttexts.org/library/celtic/jce/beansidhe.html
Joyce, P. W. (1911). The man-wolves of Ossory. Library Ireland. https://www.libraryireland.com/Wonders/Man-Wolves.php
Kaushik, N. (2011, October 24). Difference between Norse and Viking. Difference between Similar Terms and Objects. http://www.differencebetween.net/miscellaneous/culture-miscellaneous/difference-between-norse-and-viking/
Kesp, B. (2014, August 4). Tuatha Dé Danann - a Family Tree. Literature and Culture Corner. http://kespwriting.blogspot.com/2014/08/tuatha-de-danann-family-tree.html
Klein, C. (2018, September 4). Globetrotting Vikings: The raiding of Ireland. History. https://www.history.com/news/globetrotting-vikings-the-raiding-of-ireland
Klimczak, N. (2016, November 24). Bronze treasures beyond belief: The

fabulous Dowris hoard of Ireland. Ancient Origins. https://www.ancient-origins.net/artifacts-other-artifacts/bronze-treasures-beyond-belief-fabulous-dowris-hoard-ireland-007067

Knowth megalithic passage tomb. (n.d.). New Grange. https://www.newgrange.com/knowth.htm

Lancor, K., & Lancor, M. (2022, December 28). The ancient stone circles and dolmens scattered across Ireland. Irish Central. https://www.irishcentral.com/travel/ireland-ancient-stone-circles-dolmens

Leanan Sidhe. (n.d.). Encyclopedia of Occultism and Parapsychology. Encyclopedia.com. https://www.encyclopedia.com/science/encyclopedias-almanacs-transcripts-and-maps/leanan-sidhe

Leeming, D. (2006). Nemain. The Oxford Companion to World Mythology. Oxford University Press. https://www.oxfordreference.com/display/10.1093/oi/authority.20110810105455960

Life in Celtic Ireland – Ancient to modern Celticism. (2022, March 14). Connolly Cove. https://www.connollycove.com/life-in-celtic-ireland-ancient-to-modern/

Lir. (n.d.). Bard Mythologies. https://bardmythologies.com/lir/

Little, B. (2021, September 9). 5 Iron Age tools and innovations. History. https://www.history.com/news/iron-age-tools-innovations

Longáin, S. Ó. (2022, December 9). The púca (pooka) in Irish folklore. Your Irish Culture. https://www.yourirish.com/folklore/irish-pookas

Lucharacháin. (n.d.). An Sionnach Fionn. https://ansionnachfionn.com/seanchas-mythology/lucharachain/

Luchtaine. (n.d.). Academic Kids. http://academickids.com/encyclopedia/index.php/Luchta

mac Cecht. (2022). Wikipedia. Retrieved February 11, 2023 from https://en.wikipedia.org/wiki/mac_Cecht

mac Mathúna, L. (Ed.). (2021). Éigse: A journal of Irish studies (Vol. 41). National University of Ireland. chrome-extension://efaidnbmnnnibpcajpcglclefindmkaj/http://www.nui.ie/eigse/pdf/vol41/Eigse_Vol_XLI_2021_Mills.pdf

macalister, R. A. S. (1918). Pre-Celtic Ireland. The Irish Monthly, 46(536), 86–95. JStor. https://www.jstor.org/stable/20504982

macha. (n.d.). Bard Mythologies. https://bardmythologies.com/macha/

mackenzie, L. (2018, May 15). Who were the Normans and why did they conquer England? History Hit. https://www.historyhit.com/who-were-the-normans-and-why-did-they-conquer-england/#:~:text=The%20Normans%20were%20Vikings%20who

macKillop, J. (2004a). Banba. A Dictionary of Celtic Mythology. Oxford University Press. https://www.oxfordreference.com/display/10.1093/oi/authority.20110803095444436

macKillop, J. (2004b). Bodb. A Dictionary of Celtic Mythology. Oxford University Press.

https://www.oxfordreference.com/display/10.1093/oi/authority.20110803095514712

macKillop, J. (2004c). Caoránach. A Dictionary of Celtic Mythology. https://www.oxfordreference.com/display/10.1093/oi/authority.20110803095547214

macKillop, J. (2004d). Domnu. A Dictionary of Celtic Mythology. Oxford University Press. https://www.oxfordreference.com/display/10.1093/oi/authority.20110803095726564

macKillop, J. (2004e). Elmar. A Dictionary of Celtic Mythology. Oxford University Press. https://www.oxfordreference.com/display/10.1093/oi/authority.20110803095745503

macKillop, J. (2004f). Ernmas. A Dictionary of Celtic Mythology. Oxford University Press. https://www.oxfordreference.com/display/10.1093/oi/authority.20110810104841717

macKillop, J. (2004g). Fódla. A Dictionary of Celtic Mythology. Oxford University Press. https://www.oxfordreference.com/display/10.1093/oi/authority.20110803095825980

macKillop, J. (2004h). Indech. A Dictionary of Celtic Mythology. Oxford University Press. https://www.oxfordreference.com/display/10.1093/oi/authority.20110803100000698

macKillop, J. (2004i). Luchta. A Dictionary of Celtic Mythology. Oxford University Press. https://www.oxfordreference.com/display/10.1093/oi/authority.20110803100117787

macKillop, J. (2004j). Nemedians. A Dictionary of Celtic Mythology. Oxford University Press. https://www.oxfordreference.com/display/10.1093/oi/authority.20110803100228273

macKillop, J. (2004k). Overview: Brí Léith. A Dictionary of Celtic Mythology. Oxford University Press. https://www.oxfordreference.com/display/10.1093/oi/authority.20110803095527570;jsessionid=0C049D44D19452CE696BCDAA24991D25?rskey=UMDSU5&result=11

macKillop, J. (2004k). Tethra. A Dictionary of Celtic Mythology. Oxford University Press. https://www.oxfordreference.com/display/10.1093/oi/authority.20110803103251488

Mag Tuired. (2018). Encyclopedia Britannica. https://www.britannica.com/topic/Mag-Tuired

Magan, M. (2017, August 9). Fairy forts: Why these "sacred places" deserve our respect. The Irish Times. https://www.irishtimes.com/culture/heritage/fairy-forts-why-these-sacred-places-deserve-our-respect-1.3181259

Magan, M. (2021, March 13). From ringfort to ring road: The destruction of Ireland's fairy forts. The Irish Times. https://www.irishtimes.com/culture/heritage/from-ringfort-to-

ring-road-the-destruction-of-ireland-s-fairy-forts-1.4496069
Manannán mac Lir. (2006, December 27). Encyclopedia Britannica. https://www.britannica.com/topic/Manannan-mac-Lir
Mark, J. J. (2015). Ancient Ireland. World History Encyclopedia. https://www.worldhistory.org/ireland/
Mark, J. J. (2018). Kingdom of West Francia. World History Encyclopedia. https://www.worldhistory.org/Kingdom_of_West_Francia/
Martinsson-Wallin, H. (n.d.). Monuments and people - An introduction. Studies in Global Archaeology, 20. chrome-extension://efaidnbmnnnibpcajpcglclefindmkaj/https://www.diva-portal.org/smash/get/diva2:926765/FULLTEXT01.pdf
McCormick, K. (2017, October 9). Dragons of Fame: Ollipeist/Ollepheist/Ollipheist/Uilepheist. The Circle of the Dragon. http://www.blackdrago.com/fame/ollipeist.htm
McKeown, M. (2022, July 17). Forgotten fairies of Irish folklore. Owlcation. https://owlcation.com/humanities/Forgotten-Irish-Fairies
McNamara, R. (2020, January 29). Irish history: The 1800s. ThoughtCo. https://www.thoughtco.com/irish-history-the-1800s-1773853
McNamara-Wilson, K. (n.d.). Irish faerie folk of yore and yesterday – The gancanagh. Got Ireland. http://gotireland.com/2013/10/04/irish-faerie-folk-of-yore-and-yesterday-the-gancanagh/
Medieval Ireland and early Gaelic Ireland. (n.d.). Discovering Ireland. https://www.discoveringireland.com/early-gaelic-ireland-and-medieval-ireland/
Megalithic Ireland. (n.d.). Megalithic Ireland. http://www.megalithicireland.com/
Mesolithic Stone Age in prehistoric Ireland. (n.d.). Travel through the Ireland Story. https://www.wesleyjohnston.com/users/ireland/past/pre_norman_history/mesolithic_age.html
Midir. (n.d.). Bard Mythologies. https://bardmythologies.com/midir/
Military History. (2022, November 7). Born in blood: the Irish Free State. The Past. https://the-past.com/feature/born-in-blood-the-irish-free-state/
Moloney, C. (2011, February 16). Know thy monuments: Barrow/tumulus. Know Thy Place Blog. https://knowthyplace.wordpress.com/2011/02/16/know-thy-monuments-barrowtumulus/
Moody, S. (2022, March 31). Meanwhile, in Ireland: Ostara. The Comenian. https://comenian.org/7527/news/meanwhile-in-ireland-ostara/
Morus-Baird, G. (2022, August 2). The goddess of sovereignty. Celtic Source. https://celticsource.online/the-goddess-of-sovereignty/
Mould, D. P. (2001). The sailing-ships of Ancient Ireland. Archaeology Ireland, 15(1), 14–18. Jstor. https://www.jstor.org/stable/20562472
Mount, C. (2011, August 9). The houses of the Irish copper age 1.1. Dr.

Charles Mount. http://charles-mount.ie/wp/index.php/the-houses-of-the-irish-copper-age/#:~:text=In%20Ireland%20the%20use%20of
Mythology Storyteller. (2021). Celtic gods and goddesses of mythology. [Video]. YouTube. https://www.youtube.com/watch?v=BalDcKUb0DQ
Mythology Unleashed. (2022). Monsters of Celtic mythology. [Video]. YouTube. https://www.youtube.com/watch?v=OeyP8tAMWsE
Native games of Ireland. (n.d.). Mayo Ireland. https://www.mayo-ireland.ie/en/about-mayo/sports/native-games-of-ireland.html
Nave, R. (n.d.). Atmospheric refraction. Hyper Physics. http://hyperphysics.phy-astr.gsu.edu/hbase/atmos/mirage.html
Neary, C. (2021, May 30). The Irish folklore of the Celtic merrow. Beach Combing. https://www.beachcombingmagazine.com/blogs/news/the-irish-folklore-of-the-celtic-merrow#:~:text=Merrow%20(from%20the%20Irish%20Muruch
Nechtan - God of the Underworld. (n.d.). The White Goddess. http://www.thewhitegoddess.co.uk/divinity_of_the_day/irish/nechtan.asp
Nemid (or Nemed) and the Nemedians in Ireland. (1884). The Irish Fireside, 2(30). Library Ireland. https://www.libraryireland.com/articles/NemidIF2-30/index.php
Norman invasion of Ireland. (n.d.). New World Encyclopedia. https://www.newworldencyclopedia.org/entry/Norman_invasion_of_Ireland
Norman Ireland. (n.d.). New World Encyclopedia. https://www.newworldencyclopedia.org/entry/Norman_Ireland
Nuada. (2017). Encyclopedia Britannica. https://www.britannica.com/topic/Nuadu
Nugent, L. (2022, September 26). Mountains, wells, and caves: A look at Ireland's sacred landscape. The Irish Spirit. https://theirishspirit.com/mountains-wells-and-caves-a-look-at-irelands-sacred-landscape/
O'Cathasaigh, L. (2030, September 9). Tír Na nÓg - The legend of the land of eternal youth. Irish Central. https://www.irishcentral.com/roots/history/tir-na-nog-legend-eternal-youth
O'Hara, K. (2023a, January 4). The abhartach: The terrifying tale of the Irish vampire. The Irish Road Trip. https://www.theirishroadtrip.com/the-abhartach/
O'Hara, K. (2023b, January 4). The legend of the Fianna: Some of the mightiest warriors from Irish mythology. The Irish Road Trip. https://www.theirishroadtrip.com/the-fianna/
O'Keeffe, C. (n.d.). Monster/faery page. Tartan Place. http://www.tartanplace.com/faery/goddess/aeb.html
O'Neill, B. (2020, March 2). Saint Finnian of Clonard. Your Irish Culture. https://www.yourirish.com/history/christianity/st-finnian-of-clonard
O'Raifeartaigh, T. (2022). St. Patrick. Encyclopedia Britannica.

https://www.britannica.com/biography/Saint-Patrick
Odekirk, S. (2021, January 29). A look at Irish culture and traditions. Family Search. https://www.familysearch.org/en/blog/irish-culture-and-traditions
Ogma. (2015). Encyclopedia Britannica. https://www.britannica.com/topic/Ogma
Onchwari, G., & Keengwe, J. (n.d.). What is an ethnolinguistic group? In Handbook of Research on Engaging Immigrant Families and Promoting Academic Success for English Language Learners. University of North Dakota. https://www.igi-global.com/dictionary/ethnolinguistic-group/72624
Orthostat. (n.d.). Collins. https://www.collinsdictionary.com/dictionary/english/orthostat#:~:text=orthostat%20in%20American%20English,lower%20part%20of%20the%20cella
Ossory. (2020). Encyclopedia Britannica. https://www.britannica.com/place/Ossory
Overly Sarcastic Productions. (2019). History summarized: Ireland. [Video]. YouTube. https://www.youtube.com/watch?v=RCCUEt8S61k
Paciorek, A. L. (n.d.). Solitary fays. Strange Lands. http://www.batcow.co.uk/strangelands/solitary.htm
Parable - Religious History Documentaries. (2020). The mysterious world of the Celtic gods | Lost gods | Parable. [Video]. YouTube. https://www.youtube.com/watch?v=NZ0n-IW8VSg&t=11s
Parkes, V. (2018, July 28). Grange stone circle: A place of ritual gatherings, sacrifice and worship from prehistoric times to the modern day. Ancient Origins. https://www.ancient-origins.net/ancient-places-europe/grange-stone-circle-021993
Passage tomb people. (n.d.). Passage Tomb People. https://passagetombpeople.com/
Perkins, M. (2019, September 24). Irish mythology: History and legacy. Thought Co. https://www.thoughtco.com/irish-mythology-4768762
Petruzzello, M. (2022). St. Brigid of Ireland. Encyclopedia Britannica. https://www.britannica.com/biography/Saint-Brigit-of-Ireland
Prehistoric Ireland. (n.d.). National Museum of Ireland. https://www.museum.ie/en-IE/Museums/Archaeology/Exhibitions/Prehistoric-Ireland
Prehistoric monuments. (n.d.). Heritage Ireland. https://heritageireland.ie/visit/prehistoric-monuments/#:~:text=Our%20prehistoric%20monuments%20include%20Stone
Prehistoric period (until 1050 AD) / The Viking Age. (n.d.). National Museum of Denmark. https://en.natmus.dk/historical-knowledge/denmark/prehistoric-period-until-1050-ad/the-viking-age/
Quenching. (1998, July 20). Encyclopedia Britannica. https://www.britannica.com/technology/quenching-materials-processing
Quintanilla, M. (2010). Review of the book Ireland, slavery and anti-

slavery: 1612–1865 Review of Review of the book Ireland, slavery and anti-slavery: 1612–1865, by N. Rodgers. New Hibernia Review, 14(4), 153–154. muse.jhu.edu/article/412036.

Radford, B. (2017, March 8). Leprechauns: Facts about the Irish trickster fairy. Live Science. https://www.livescience.com/37626-leprechauns.html

Rafferty, J. P. (2022). Neolithic. Encyclopædia Britannica. https://www.britannica.com/event/Neolithic

Rafferty, R. (2021, May 30). The myths and legends of Ireland's hound of deep, the dobhar chu. Irish Central. https://www.irishcentral.com/roots/irelands-hound-dobhar-chu

Rainbolt, D. (2022, January 20). The wee folk of Ireland. Wilderness Ireland. https://www.wildernessireland.com/blog/irish-folklore-fairies/

Ring fort. (n.d.). Britannica Kids. https://kids.britannica.com/kids/article/ring-fort/487545

Ryan, W. G. (n.d.). A survey of monuments of archaeological and historical interest in the Barony of Bunratty Lower, Co. Clare. Clare Country Library. https://www.clarelibrary.ie/eolas/coclare/archaeology/ryan/part1_ring_barrows.htm#:~:text=In%20general%20ring%2Dbarrows%20may

Samhain. (2022, October 5). History. https://www.history.com/topics/holidays/samhain#:~:text=Ancient%20Celts%20marked%20Samhain%20as

See U in History / Mythology. (2022). Irish mythology: The arrival of the Celtic gods - Complete - The Tuatha Dé Danann - See u in history. [Video]. YouTube. https://www.youtube.com/watch?v=mwLuVo3N1fY&t=19s

Shaw, J. (2014, January 30). Etain, the shining one – Celtic sun goddess/goddess of transformation by Judith Shaw. Feminism and Religion. https://feminismandreligion.com/2014/01/30/etain-the-shining-one-celtic-sun-goddess-by-judith-shaw/

Sleeping Ulstermen. (n.d.). Bard Mythologies. https://bardmythologies.com/sleeping-ulstermen/

Sluagh. (n.d.). Emerald Isle. https://emeraldisle.ie/sluagh

Snell, M. (2021, February 17). The Early, High, and Late Middle Ages. ThoughtCo. https://www.thoughtco.com/defining-the-middle-ages-part-6-1788883

St. Enda. (n.d.). Catholic News Agency. https://www.catholicnewsagency.com/saint/st-enda-700

Standing stones. (n.d.). As about Ireland. https://www.askaboutireland.ie/reading-room/environment-geography/physical-landscape/man-and-the-landscape-in/dun-laoghaire-rathdown-ea/megalithic-monuments-4/#:~:text=Standing%20Stone%2C%20Glencullen%20(location)

Stone Age. (n.d.). National Museum of Ireland. https://www.museum.ie/en-ie/collections-research/irish-antiquities-division-collections/collections-list-(1)/stone-age

Stone, R., & Winters, R. (2019, March 22). The wooing of Etain: An Irish tale of love, loss, and jealousy. Ancient Origins.

https://www.ancient-origins.net/myths-legends-europe/wooing-etain-irish-tale-love-loss-and-jealousy-003077

Study of antiquity and the Middle Ages. (2022). Irish origins | The genetic history of Ireland. [Video]. YouTube. https://www.youtube.com/watch?v=HxivGM_LESk&t=641s

Subtracting insult from injury: the medical judgements of the Brehon Law. (n.d.). History Ireland. https://www.historyireland.com/subtracting-insult-from-injury-he-medical-judgements-of-the-brehon-law/#:~:text=The%20Brehon%20Law%20was%20the,complexity%20of%20early%20Irish%20society.

Suibhne. (2017). The animated history of Ireland. [Video]. YouTube. https://www.youtube.com/watch?v=dQvaGt9B6H0&t=488s

Teutates. (2018). Encyclopedia Britannica. https://www.britannica.com/topic/Teutates

The adventures of Connla the Fair. (1936). T. P. Cross & C. H. Slover (Trans.), Ancient Irish Tales. Henry Holt & Co. https://www.maryjones.us/ctexts/connla.html

The Bodach. (n.d.). Emerald Isle. https://emeraldisle.ie/the-bodach

The Bronze Age. (n.d.). Travel through the Ireland Story. https://www.wesleyjohnston.com/users/ireland/past/pre_norman_history/summary2.htm#:~:text=The%20Bronze%20Age%20in%20Ireland

The Bronze Age in Ireland. (n.d.). National Museum of Ireland. https://microsites.museum.ie/bronzeagehandlingbox/bronze-age.html

The Celts. (n.d.). Knowth. https://www.knowth.com/celts.htm

The chase of Slieve Faud. (1920). Old Celtic romances (pp. 362–385). The Educational Company of Ireland. https://storyarchaeology.com/wp-content/uploads/The_Chase_of_Slieve_Fuad=Joyce.rtf

The Cú Sidhe. (n.d.). Emerald Isle. https://emeraldisle.ie/the-cu-sidhe

The demna aeoir. (n.d.). Emerald Isle. https://emeraldisle.ie/the-demna-aeoir

The dream of Aengus. (n.d.). Mythopedia. https://mythopedia.com/topics/aengus

The fear gorta. (n.d.). Emerald Isle. https://emeraldisle.ie/the-fear-gorta

The four jewels or treasures of the Tuatha Dé Danann. (2016, May 11). An Sionnach Fionn. https://ansionnachfionn.com/2016/05/12/the-four-jewels-or-treasures-of-the-tuatha-de-danann/

The great wyrms of Ireland. (n.d.). Emerald Isle. https://emeraldisle.ie/the-great-wyrms-of-ireland

The Histocrat. (2020). The druids. [Video]. YouTube. https://www.youtube.com/watch?v=8JBW-_zq4xM&t=4781s

The history of Ireland: 11 milestone moments. (2019, February 5). HistoryExtra. https://www.historyextra.com/period/20th-century/the-history-of-ireland-11-milestone-moments/

The Irish Jewelry Company. (2022, August 10). Celebrating the Autumn equinox called Mabon. Irish Culture and Traditions.

https://irishcultureandtraditions.org/2022/08/10/celebrating-the-autumn-equinox-called-mabon/
The last dragon in Ireland. (N.d.). Emerald Isle. https://emeraldisle.ie/the-last-dragon-in-ireland
The legend lives on. (n.d.). Old Church Visitor Centre. https://www.oldchurchvisitorcentre.com/about/tuatha-de-danann-clan
The Legend of the selkies | Ultimate mythology blog - top selkie facts. (2022, June 24). Connolly Cove. https://www.connollycove.com/the-legend-of-the-selkies/
The Neolithic, or New Stone Age. (n.d.). Travel through the Ireland Story. https://www.wesleyjohnston.com/users/ireland/past/pre_norman_history/neolithic_age.html
The ninety-seven Kerbstones at Newgrange. (n.d.). The Fr. O'Flanagan Heritage Centre. http://www.carrowkeel.com/sites/boyne/newkerbstones.html
The Protestant Ascendency. (n.d.). Discovering Ireland. https://www.discoveringireland.com/the-protestant-ascendency/
The Red Branch knights. (1906). A smaller social history of ancient Ireland. Longmans, Green, and Co. https://www.libraryireland.com/SocialHistoryAncientIreland/I-III-3.php
The River Boyne. (n.d.). Boyne Valley Tours. https://boynevalleydaytours.com/boyne-river.htm
The Roman Empire in the first century: Early Christians. (n.d.). Public Broadcasting Service. https://www.pbs.org/empires/romans/empire/christians.html#:~:text=In%20313%20AD%2C%20the%20Emperor
The Storm Hag. (n.d.). Emerald Isle. https://emeraldisle.ie/the-storm-hag
The voyage of Bran. (n.d.). Bard Mythologies. https://bardmythologies.com/voyage-of-bran/
The water horse. (n.d.). Emerald Isle. https://emeraldisle.ie/the-water-horse
Thomond. (2022, November 3). Wikipedia. Retrieved December 24, 2022 from https://en.wikipedia.org/wiki/Thomond
Thompson, T. F. (n.d.). Ireland's pre-Celtic archaeological and anthropological heritage. Knowth. https://www.knowth.com/ireland_pre-celtic.htm
Timeline - World History Documentaries. (2021). The mysteries of the Celtic Otherworld | Myths and monsters | Timeline. [Video]. YouTube. https://www.youtube.com/watch?v=iuKVQHyWxqA&t=14s
Toner, E. (2019). The secret world of life (and death) in Ireland's peat bogs. The New York Times. https://www.nytimes.com/interactive/2019/10/19/multimedia/ireland-peat-bogs.html
Tuatha Dé Danann. (2023). Wikipedia. Retrieved February 10, 2023 from https://en.wikipedia.org/wiki/Tuatha_D%C3%A9_Danann
Tuatha Dé Danann. (2023, January 27). Encyclopedia Britannica.

https://www.britannica.com/topic/Tuatha-De-Danann

Tudor conquest of Ireland. (2023). Wikipedia. Retrieved February 5, 2023 from https://en.wikipedia.org/wiki/Tudor_conquest_of_Ireland

Tudor Ireland. (n.d.). Ask about Ireland. https://www.askaboutireland.ie/learning-zone/secondary-students/history/tudor-ireland/

Uyeno, G. (2019, June 10). What are rock cairns? Live Science. https://www.livescience.com/65687-rock-cairns.html

VendettaVixen. (2022, August 23). Types of Irish fairies: Leprechauns, grogochs, and other species. Exemplore. https://exemplore.com/magic/typesofirishfairies

Viking. (2022). A. Augustyn (Ed.), Encyclopedia Britannica. https://www.britannica.com/topic/Viking-people

Walter, R., Fanning, R., Kay, S., O'Beirne Ranelagh, J., & Edwards, D. (2023). Ireland. Encyclopædia Britannica. https://www.britannica.com/place/Ireland

Webb, A. (1878). Saint Columcille. Library Ireland. https://www.libraryireland.com/biography/SaintColumcille.php

Weebush. (2020, November 17). The red cap. Ireland's Lore and Tales. https://irelandsloreandtales.com/2020/11/17/the-red-cap/

Wheel of the year. (2022). Wikipedia. Retrieved 8 February, 2023 from https://en.wikipedia.org/wiki/Wheel_of_the_Year#:~:text=The%20Wheel%20of%20the%20Year,and%20the%20midpoints%20between%20them.

Who was St. Brendan. (n.d.). St. Brendan Parish. https://www.stbrendannortholmsted.org/WhoWasStBrendan.aspx#:~:text=He%20is%20known%20as%20one

Wigington, P. (2019, June 25). The magic of stone circles. Learn Religions. https://www.learnreligions.com/what-are-stone-circles-2562648

Williams, A. (2022, November 29). Morrigan. Mythopedia. https://mythopedia.com/topics/morrigan

Wright, G. (2022a). Aengus. Mythopedia. https://mythopedia.com/topics/aengus

Wright, G. (2022b, November 29). Badb. Mythopedia. https://mythopedia.com/topics/badb

Wright, G. (2022c). Lugh. Mythopedia. https://mythopedia.com/topics/lugh

Wright, G. (2022d, November 29). Medb. Mythopedia. https://mythopedia.com/topics/medb

Wright, G. (2022e). Neit. Mythopedia. https://mythopedia.com/topics/neit

Wright, G. (2022f). Nuada. Mythopedia. https://mythopedia.com/topics/nuada

Wright, G. (2022g). Taranis. Mythopedia. https://mythopedia.com/topics/taranis

Yeats, W. B. (n.d.). Irish court cairns. The Fr. O'Flanagan Heritage Centre. http://www.carrowkeel.com/files/courtcairns.html

Young, E. (1909). The coming of Lugh: A Celtic wonder-tale. The Fr. Michael O'Flanagan History and Heritage Centre; Maunsel & Co.,

LTD. http://www.carrowkeel.com/sites/moytura/lugh.html

Zhelyazkov, Y. (n.d.). Far darrig – The leprechaun's evil cousin. Symbol Sage. https://symbolsage.com/far-darrig-celtic-mythology/

(n.d.). Ask about Ireland. https://www.askaboutireland.ie/narrative-notes/the-ice-age-in-ireland/index.xml#:~:text=This%20last%20major%20period%20of

FREE BONUS FROM HBA: EBOOK BUNDLE

Greetings!

First of all, thank you for reading our books. As fellow passionate readers of History and Mythology, we aim to create the very best books for our readers.

Now, we invite you to join our VIP list. As a welcome gift, we offer the History & Mythology Ebook Bundle below for free. Plus, you can be the first to receive new books and exclusives! <u>Remember it's 100% free to join.</u>

Simply scan the QR code to join.

OTHER BOOKS BY HISTORY BROUGHT ALIVE

Available now in Ebook, Paperback, Hardcover, and Audiobook in all regions.

History Brought Alive

For Kids:

IRISH HISTORY AND MYTHOLOGY

We sincerely hope you enjoyed our new book **"Irish History and Mythology"**. We would greatly appreciate your feedback with an honest review at the place of purchase.

First and foremost, we are always looking to grow and improve as a team. It is reassuring to hear what works, as well as receive constructive feedback on what should improve. Second, starting out as an unknown author is exceedingly difficult, and Amazon reviews go a long way toward making the journey out of anonymity possible. Please take a few minutes to write an honest review.

Best regards,
History Brought Alive
http://historybroughtalive.com/

www.ingramcontent.com/pod-product-compliance
Lightning Source LLC
Chambersburg PA
CBHW070736020526
44118CB00035B/1372